THE
QUALITY SCHOOL TEACHER

BOOKS BY WILLIAM GLASSER

The Quality School Teacher
The Quality School
Control Theory in the Classroom
Control Theory
Schools Without Failure
Reality Therapy
Positive Addiction
The Identity Society
Mental Health or Mental Illness?
Stations of the Mind

THE
QUALITY SCHOOL
TEACHER

Specific suggestions for teachers who are
trying to implement the lead-management ideas
of *The Quality School* in their classrooms

William Glasser, M.D.

HarperPerennial
A Division of HarperCollins*Publishers*

HarperCollins books may be purchased for educational, business, or sales promotional use. For information, please write: Special Markets Department, HarperCollins Publishers, Inc., 10 East 53rd Street, New York, NY 10022.

FIRST EDITION

Library of Congress Cataloging-in-Publication Data
Glasser, William, 1925–
    The quality school teacher / by William Glasser.—1st ed.
      p. cm.
    "Specific suggestions for teachers who are trying to implement the lead-management ideas of the quality school in their classrooms."
    Sequel to: The quality school. c1992.
    Includes bibliographical references.
    ISBN 0-06-095019-6
    1. Teaching. 2. Teacher-student relationships. 3. Classroom management.
4. Classroom environment. I. Glasser, William, 1925–Quality school. II. Title.
LB1025.3.G52 1993
371.1'02—dc20   92-56268

94 95 96 97 ❖/RRD 10 9 8 7 6 5

Dedication

For the past fifteen years my wife, Naomi, has edited my books and also two books of her own, What Are You Doing? *and* Control Theory in the Practice of Reality Therapy. *In all cases, her meticulous editing made what I said concise and crystal clear. If you have had the opportunity to read these books, you may not agree with me, but what she did guarantees that you had no difficulty understanding my meaning.*

It is with great sadness that I write these words, as this is the last book she had a chance to edit. She passed away from cancer in December 1992, after a brief but devastating illness. Ill as she was, she insisted on editing and was critical of herself for not being able to do what she thought was her best. I assured her, and I think that you will agree, that her work was high quality right to the end. I think when she read the final manuscript she was satisfied.

DEDICATION

I want to acknowledge here that my work would not have been of the quality that I am told it is without her dedicated help throughout a long and satisfying marriage. Those who knew her—and her friends in the schools and in the counseling profession were numerous—understand what she did and will miss her caring and dedication to the ideas we use, which have helped so many people.

When the book was finished the initial dedication was as follows:

This book is dedicated to the two school teachers in my family, my son, Martin, and his wife, Pamela. Martin is a high school history and social studies teacher, Pam teaches kindergarten. They both live and work in Connecticut.

It is only fitting that this dedication be included here. Naomi was very proud of both Martin and Pam and their decision to go into what she believed was among the highest of all occupations: teaching.

Contents

CONTENTS

Acknowledgments

I want to thank the many teachers, administrators, and staff members of the institute who have worked so hard to get these ideas started. And I wish to thank all the people who work at the institute office for their dedication to the ideas and for helping to get them understood. If you have any questions at all, call the institute. We want to hear from you and we will do everything we can to help you.

Preface

For many years very competent and dedicated people have been trying unsuccessfully to improve our schools. It is natural for you to ask the question, "Why will a Quality School succeed when almost everything else has failed?"

The answer is in the following quote from W. Edwards Deming, whom you know from reading *The Quality School* and, I am sure, from other sources. Deming is a brilliant man. If we would follow his management ideas, we would not be mired in the present economic recession. His ideas apply as much to schools as to business. He says, *"Knowledge is prediction, and knowledge comes from theory. Experience teaches nothing without theory. Do not try to copy someone else's success. Unless you understand the theory behind it, trying to copy it can lead to complete chaos."*[1]

The reason the Quality School program has a chance to succeed where other programs have failed is that it is based on a new theory, **control theory.**[2] It is the first school improvement program based on this theory. Almost all others are based on an old theory (stimulus-response) that leads to the **bossing** that is the cause of almost all our present problems both in education and industry.

Anyone who understands control theory can easily see that the programs of the few schools around the country that are succeeding are based on it, even though the people that run these schools usually do not know that this is the case. **This is why, as Deming says so clearly, their success has been so difficult to duplicate.** People who try to copy successful schools without understanding the theory behind their success will fail: a sure prescription for the present chaos in educational reform.

Any school staff willing to make the effort to learn to use control theory and to teach it to their students will succeed because **they will know why they are succeeding. Therefore, a Quality School can be duplicated by any school whose staff is willing to make the effort.** The purpose of this book is to offer teachers specific suggestions for putting the theory into practice in their classrooms.

Author's Note

The Quality School was initially published in the spring of 1990 by HarperCollins. Because of the widespread interest in the ideas, I wrote a series of reference bulletins that attempt to answer many of the questions that have been raised by teachers and administrators who are trying to implement these ideas in their schools and classrooms. These bulletins have been, and still are, available through the Institute for Reality Therapy.

After a discussion with Hugh Van Dusen, my editor at HarperCollins, we decided to include nineteen of these bulletins in the **new** edition of **The Quality School** that was published in fall, 1992. Also included in this new edition is a detailed explanation of how a school can join the Quality School Consortium in Training. The consortium is growing rapidly. If you need more information about any aspect of the Quality School, write, call, or fax:

AUTHOR'S NOTE

The Institute for Reality Therapy
7301 Medical Center Drive
Suite 104
Canoga Park, CA 91307
PHONE: (818) 888-0688; FAX: (818) 888-3023

THE
QUALITY SCHOOL TEACHER

CHAPTER ONE

Quality School Teachers Always Lead, They Never Boss

This book is addressed specifically to teachers who are working in schools where there has been tangible interest in the Quality School ideas. Because, in sharing these ideas, I feel close to you, I address you as "you" in this text. As I explain the material that follows, I am assuming you have read not only *The Quality School* but the reference bulletins that were written after the book was published in 1990. (The new 1992 edition of *The Quality School* includes almost all of these bulletins.) If you have a 1990 edition, I assume your school or district has obtained the bulletins from the Institute for Reality Therapy and made them available to you. If you haven't yet read them, you will get much more out of this book if you read them now.

I am also assuming that, if you are a member of a staff of a school that has signed the contract to become a Quality School, you have discussed much of this material in staff meetings with your principal, and **you are convinced that you have administrative support for what you are trying to do.** While I am addressing teachers from contract schools,[3] this book should also be of great help to teachers who are working in the many schools and school systems that are sympathetic to these ideas but have not yet taken the step of signing the contract.

As of fall 1993 the staffs of more than one hundred schools, having read and agreed with the ideas in *The Quality School,* have signed contracts committing themselves to move to Quality Schools. I have kept in touch with them and written the bulletins previously mentioned, but it is still apparent to me that both teachers and administrators are having great difficulty **making the major change in the system of education that has to be made if their school is to become a Quality School. They have to give up boss-managing and start lead-managing.**

If Deming were involved in this project, he would have predicted this difficulty, because it arises in almost all organizations that attempt to move to quality. The managers, which in a school would be the administrators and teachers, resist because they fear that, if they go along with what Deming says, they will have to give up power. They find it hard to realize that **it is the personal power associated with bossing that is the enemy of the quality they are trying to achieve.**

Before any school can become a Quality School, the principal has to commit to the new system—lead-management—and, by leading instead of bossing, convince the teachers that he or she has actually made the commitment. The next step is for the teachers to stop bossing and start leading their students and, in doing so, demonstrate to them that something new and better is going on in their classrooms. Both these steps are difficult steps, but, in practice, the principals have an easier job than the teachers.

The principal's main task in a Quality School is to lead-manage teachers who have already shown a strong interest in learning to do this themselves and appreciate all the help they can get as they start. Teachers, on the other hand, have to both **manage and teach** students, many of whom don't even want to be in school, and none of whom will show much interest in what system of management you use or, initially, have much interest in helping you do anything. To reach these students is what this book is all about, and to help you to do this, your principal needs to do more than allow you to change. He or she must vigorously support all you do as you try to implement the lead-management ideas in this book.

Until your students can be convinced that something new and better for them is happening in your classroom, they will not seriously consider putting forth the effort it takes to do Quality Schoolwork. Some of your students have done good schoolwork, but for almost all students quality work is a completely new idea. They have never even thought of doing it, much less done it. Initially, they will perceive quality work as being too hard, and most will resist. They will continue to resist until you teach them **first what quality is** and then **that they can do Quality Schoolwork.** This will be your main task as a Quality School teacher.

The most powerful thing you can do to convince your students that something new is in place is to talk to them much more than most of you have ever done before. As you talk to them, in a variety of ways, tell them that it is **their school,** not your school, the principal's school, or their parents' school. By their school, you mean that nothing is going to be forced upon them, that together you will agree on what is useful to learn, and that you will work with them to solve all problems because, if it is their school, the problems are their problems. You will have to work hard to prevent them from turning their problems over to you, as they are used to doing.

To do this best, you will have to get rid of the standard rectangular classroom configuration of rows and **change to a new configuration, a circle, with you as a part of it.** The purpose of the circle is for you to be able, on a moment's notice, to get their attention and start discussing anything that is important. In the standard arrangement, unless you are a communications genius, you cannot reach beyond the first two rows. If you can't reach them, they will never be willing to accept that this is their school. I am aware that there will be tremendous resistance to changing the way students sit. You should clear this with your principal and then be prepared to sweet-talk your custodian for a number of weeks if you want to get him or her to go along.

As you are already aware from what I have written, the success of our boss-managed, traditional schools, where few students perceive ownership, is much more related to the homes the students come from than to what happens in school. Even this success is not high. In the best schools, which means schools where there is the most family support, no more than half the students do good work: Almost none do quality work. In communities where there is little family support for education, the number of students who do good work may drop to as low as 5 percent: Quality work is almost nonexistent. The goal of a Quality School is all students doing some quality work. The school, as much as or more than the family, has to convince the students that it is a worthwhile effort.

Until the late 1970s, the majority of our political leaders were satisfied with our schools. There was no pressure to fix what did not seem to be broken. Now, very suddenly, they have become aware that not nearly enough students get good grades or score well on achievement tests. This awareness has led to the present hue and cry to improve the schools. But there is no hue and cry for quality. The pressure is to improve achievement on mass tests, but even this has failed because, so far, almost all the suggested improvements are tied to **the old teach, test, reward, and punish, boss-managed system.**

After twenty years of unsuccessful struggle, all we have accumulated is a pile of evidence that our traditional boss-managed system has taken the schools as far as it can. If we do not change from bossing to leading, the schools will not improve by any standard, even the nonstandard of low-quality, mass achievement tests. But worst of all, the students will not learn to do the quality work they must do if our society is to be economically competitive in the 1990s. We do not have the luxury of planning for a distant future: We must make these changes now.

Even most of the schools that say they are now trying to follow Deming or have embraced the wonderful sounding acronym TQM (total quality management) are getting nowhere, because their administrators and school boards seem unable to understand that, to use Deming's ideas successfully, **they have to do as he says: "Change the system!"** Educators are far from alone in their inability to understand Deming. The reluctance to accept that the system must be changed also extends to leaders of industry, many of whom have recently become involved with the schools.

In their call for more testing, coupled with the implied threat that schools that do not measure up will be punished or shut down, most of these businessmen turned educators cling to the worst features of boss-management, strong evidence that they have missed Deming's main point. **Whether the failure to achieve quality is in industry or education, nothing will be improved until the leaders change the system itself.**

It is never the fault of the people who work in the system.

To try to help you to see what I mean, let me use a simple household example of how difficult it is to change from an old system to a new one. Almost all of you are aware of the claims that are made for new dishwashers: You do not have to do anything more than scrape off the loose food before you put them in to wash. We all know that most people with a new dishwasher do much more than scrape; they prewash the dishes before putting them in the machine. They do this because they have always done it. They are not able to conceptualize that these new machines are equipped with a new dishwashing system that is capable of doing exactly what is claimed. So they keep prewashing by hand, sticking to the old system, because they cannot conceptualize the new.

While it is much more complicated, the problem of moving from bossing to leading is the same as giving up prewashing. If you can accept the ideas of Deming and control theory and then lead-manage and lead-teach accordingly, all students will begin to do good work and discipline problems will disappear. It is hard to believe this is true. Just as many of our industrial leaders, whose industries make low-quality products and are failing to compete, cannot conceptualize Deming enough to stop boss-managing, too many teachers are also stuck in the old system.

For example, teachers who are trying to use the new Quality School lead-managing system keep asking, "But what do I do if I don't punish them when they don't do the work I assign?" Instead of accepting the idea that all students not only can but will begin to do better work (better in the beginning, quality later) if they are not punished or threatened, they keep asking the same question and keep punishing. They cannot conceptualize the control theory that underlies lead-management, which is that their students are not doing the assigned work because they do not find it need-satisfying. Following the old boss-managed system, teachers can't rid their minds of the thought, "I know what I tell them to do is good for them. They ought to do it whether they like it or not."

I am well aware, however, that teachers who really want to change are not staying with the old system because they are stubborn. They simply don't know enough about the new system to get a working understanding of what it is. To help them, I have written a lot, but it is still not enough. Deming has the same problem. He is ninety-three years old and can cite as examples many businesses in Japan to prove that what he says works in industry; still, he has been much less successful than he would like to be in this country.[4]

I wish we had a large, successful school model comparable to what he has with business in Japan, but we do not. Some of the schools that have signed the contract are getting close, however. It is encouraging that he and I are busy explaining quality management over and over to people in this country: These people are aware that they need new ideas desperately. It is discouraging that

8

so many people are so stuck in the old system that they seem unable to catch on to the fact that, if quality is what is wanted, it is obsolete.

To change a traditional system, such as how we manage people, is a massive job. It requires much more than any of us think is necessary. The salesperson who sold you the new dishwasher could come to your house every night for a week, put the barely scraped dishes in, wait until they are washed, take them out sparkling clean, and ask you to begin doing what you have just seen with your own eyes, and you would still have difficulty doing it. If you are not vigilant, you will slip back into the prewashing that you've done for years. If you start the move to lead-managing, it will take even more vigilance to keep from slipping back to old, coercive ways to teach.

Because the boss-managed school is much more fixed in your heads than prewashing dishes, the main thrust of this book is to suggest several specific teaching practices that will help you to lead-manage. I realize that much of what I am going to offer will be new to you, but **it has to be** if it is to work in the new system. What should be encouraging is that, in the experience of professionals like yourselves who have tried them, these practices are easier and more enjoyable than what you are doing now.

The only way education is going to change is if the classroom teacher makes it happen. Here at the beginning, I want to emphasize that what I recommend, even urge, are suggestions: Nothing in this book should be considered mandatory. Using my knowledge of both control theory and Deming, I will try to explain the reasons for what I suggest and make clear why it has a good chance of working for you. If what I have written makes sense, think about it, and then slowly and carefully try to put it into practice. There is no hurry. It takes time to become a Quality School teacher.

CHAPTER TWO

The Quality School Teacher Is a Professional

Assuming you will be managed by administrators who understand what a Quality School is, almost all of you will find that, for the first time in your career, you will have the opportunity to be a professional teacher. In any field, and this certainly should include teaching school, professionals not only know how to do the job they are hired to do, but they are also given an opportunity to do that job the way they believe is best. For example, if you are hired as a professional to teach fifth grade, you will make sure that you are clear on what you are expected to accomplish, but you will be equally sure that you will be given the opportunity to use your professional skills to do so.

Therefore, how a professional accomplishes the job is up to that person. This does not mean that you are not open to suggestions and learning new and better ways to practice your profession, but it does mean that you are not compelled to follow anyone's lead except your own. Within the boundaries of your assignment, you figure out your own curriculum, use the materials you think are best in the way you believe is most effective, use any method of teaching, such as cooperative learning, that you think will work, and figure out how to evaluate your students so that they show you, themselves, and anyone else that they have learned what they are supposed to learn in your class. In short, if you accept the assignment, it is yours to accomplish.

The most important difference between professionals and nonprofessionals in any field goes far beyond being able to do the job without outside direction: It is that professionals are interested in quality. The work they do themselves is quality, and, if they manage or teach others, it is important to them that they do quality work. Getting the job done, even done well, is good enough for nonprofessionals, but continually improving the way the job is done both for themselves and others is the hallmark of professionals.

A professional teacher would not ask any student to do anything that is not quality, so all of the nonsensical memorizing that teachers now require their students to do would be absent from a Quality School. Teaching public school students so that they do quality work is almost nonexistent in our schools, where teachers and students are boss-managed. If this is to be accomplished it will only be through the leadership of professional teachers who make the effort to learn to become lead-managers.

As traditional schools operate now, teachers are not treated as professionals. Everyone, administrators, school boards, state departments, and the legislature, and the governors' offices, has a hand in telling teachers what they want done, how to do it, and how it will be measured. There is no job that requires professionals more than teaching, yet there is no job in which the people who do it are treated in ways that make it impossible for them to be professional. Imagine what medicine or law would be like if physicians and lawyers were treated as teachers are. Teaching well is certainly much more difficult than performing well in either of these more respected professions.

A high school science teacher in one of our contract schools told me that for the first time in his career he is acting as a professional. His principal is encouraging him and all of her teachers to teach the way they think is best. He has decided to follow many of the suggestions in *The Quality School,* and he says the results are phenomenal: All his students are learning science enthusiastically and doing better work than they have ever done before, even quality work. But he is worried because he is not covering as much as he tried to cover in the past (actually, he never succeeded, because it was too much to cover), and he tells me that he fears he will be fired if his present principal leaves and is replaced by a traditional principal.

Although I doubt it will happen, I agreed that it could. In a lighter vein, I also said that if he feels threatened by a new principal, he knows how to teach unprofessionally, how to turn students off and spend his time dealing with discipline problems (these have all disappeared); if he has to, he can go back to where he was. He smiled and said he'll take his chances with what he is doing now. Most of what he is saying is that it takes a while to get comfortable with a new system. He had taught the old system for fifteen years, the new one for less than a year. He was also using his fear to brag a little about what he has accomplished. He has every right to be proud of it.

What he is saying is more complicated than it seems. Why is he one of the few teachers out of a large faculty (over seventy teachers), all of whom have the opportunity to do what he has done, who have not availed themselves of lead-management to the extent he has? The answer is that it is hard to do, and that was why he was bragging a little. As much as many teachers say they want to be treated as professionals, when it happens, as it will in a Quality School, it is not going to be easy.

It is much easier to chafe against all the constraints, to gripe about the inadequate textbooks, the unfair state tests, the mandated coverage of so much ground, and the strong suggestion that some ways to teach are preferred over others. This is easier than to accept the responsibility to change. Teachers will have many difficult adjustments to make when they are given the opportunity to become professionals and move from bossing to leading. This book is addressed to teachers who, given the opportunity, want to become professionals.

In a Quality School, if asked, it would be your responsibility as a professional teacher to write out a brief summary of what you propose to teach and how you propose to show that your students have learned what you are teaching them to the point of beginning to do some quality work. These summaries would be available to other teachers to help coordinate what each is teaching and to avoid duplication. It should still be your professional responsibility to teach in a way that is acceptable to the community, just as a physician is responsible to practice in a way that is not unusual or unproven in his community.

Because no one's life is at stake, a teacher should be allowed much more leeway than a physician. Still, when you do something new or unusual in your classroom, it would be good to prepare your principal and maybe explain what you are doing to some of your key, supportive parents. For example, in a Quality School there is a strong mandate to eliminate compulsory homework, because almost no students do quality homework when it is compulsory. But because homework is such a sacred cow, you would be well advised to work together as a staff to figure out how best to introduce the new procedure and to explain to skeptical parents that, given the opportunity to improve what they do and to work toward quality, students are usually more than willing to do some of the work at home.

To gain parental support for new practices, ask your parents to keep you posted on how their children like the new system and to keep track of instances in which they see their child doing more and better work than before. A Quality School teacher not only completely eliminates the adversarial relationship with students that is universal in the old system but makes sure that parents are well informed that this is what is going on. The best way to do this is to ask students to tell you in class discussions what they have learned that they believe is useful. It may take a while, but when they are able to do this, give them a homework assignment to tell their parents what they learned. Nothing will gain you more parental support than parents hearing from an enthusiastic child that he or she has learned something useful in school.

Parents, too, should be involved in a program in which they are taught what you are now doing and how they can do much the same as they teach and manage their children at home. The more you can teach them to be supportive and to avoid the adversarial relationship that often exists because they nag, punish, and reward their children for doing schoolwork, the easier their children will be to teach.

At this point don't concern yourself further about what being a professional means. The whole book will be devoted to this issue, and, as I go along, it will become increasingly clear.

CHAPTER THREE

The Six Conditions of Quality

It has become apparent to me that to teach so your students do quality work, you need a much better understanding of quality than I have provided in what I have written so far. To begin, what we all need to realize is that, past infancy, what is most important for all of us is the quality of our lives. **Any government, organization, system, business, or family that does not succeed in helping the people it serves, manages, persuades, sells to, or loves to increase the quality of their lives will either fail or be unable to compete successfully with one that does.**

Few students in traditional schools do quality work, because they do not believe that **what** they are asked to do and/or **how** they are asked to do it does anything to improve the quality of their lives. This does not end with the students. Teachers, when they are not treated as professionals (and almost none are), also do not believe that what they are asked to do and/or how they are asked to do it increases the quality of their lives.

It is also common knowledge that many parents and members of the community the schools serve do not believe that what goes on in local schools increases the quality of their lives. Turning this unfortunate situation around so that students, teachers, parents, and community members believe that what goes on in school increases the quality of their lives is the **purpose** of Quality Schools.

It is important to understand that maintaining the quality of our lives is so vital that for many of us it can become a matter of life or death. For example, we are probably the only living creatures who, given all the means of physical survival, still may choose to commit suicide when we feel desperately lonely or powerless. We choose to die because we believe the quality of our lives is so low, and there is so little chance it will improve, that our existence is no longer tolerable.

There are few school systems in this country that have not had a child suicide. Children who have attempted suicide tell researchers that failure to perform as they or their parents wanted them to in school was a major factor in their decision to try to end their lives. This is the same as saying that, for them, there was little or no quality to what they were doing in school.

If you are to teach in a way that the quality of your students' lives is at least maintained (in a Quality School the goal would be to improve it), then it is important that I help you to get a clear understanding of what quality is. This I have not done so far. In fact, as I look over what I have written about the Quality School, I believe I have given the impression that quality is very difficult both to define and to understand. I now wish to correct this impression: **Quality, or quality of life, is difficult neither to define nor to understand.**

Control theory, even to the limited extent that it is discussed in *The Quality School,* holds that all human beings have five basic needs: **love, power, freedom, fun, and survival**. These are built into our genetic structure, and from birth we **must** devote all our behavior to attempt to satisfy them. **Quality, therefore, is anything we experience that is consistently satisfying to one or more of these basic needs.**

When we are born we do not know what these needs are or how to satisfy them. Without knowledge of control theory, most of us never learn precisely what they are, but to some extent all of us learn how to satisfy them. This is because, at birth, we are all capable of knowing what feels good, what feels bad, and the difference between the two. Immediately after birth, we become aware that it is better to feel good than bad and quickly learn that it feels good to eat—all **survival** behaviors feel good. Almost immediately we also learn that it feels good **to be loved** and, later, **to love.** Based on our ability to feel good, we also learn how important it is to have **fun,** to be **free,** and to have some control over what happens to us and around us, which is **power.** As we grow older and more experienced, almost all of us learn that satisfying our needs takes planning, hard work, and patience. To the extent you can teach this to your students, they will have learned a lesson that will serve them all their lives.

It is obvious we don't have to know control theory to figure out it is worth trying to live our lives so that most of the time we feel good. Most of us are aware that a quality life is desirable even if we know nothing about the basic needs. But if you are a teacher in a Quality School, knowing the control theory and teaching it to your students will help both you and them to do what needs to be done to increase the quality of your lives. In a traditional school this does not happen for far too many students and teachers; in a Quality School, this is the goal. To achieve that goal, neither staff nor students will ever be asked to do anything that does not have a chance of improving the quality of their lives.

What I have just explained about quality and the needs is accurate and worth knowing, but this brief the-oretical explanation is not specific enough for you to put into practice in your classroom. What I want to do in this chapter is expand the theory with an explanation of quality that you can use as you teach, so that you can easily tell whether or not you are on the right track.

To do this, **I have developed six specific conditions of Quality Schoolwork that you can use to guide your teaching.** If these conditions become a part of all you do in your classroom, your students will begin to do Qual-ity Schoolwork, and they will do it because they enjoy school. While I believe that these conditions are clear and understandable, I am aware that they will not be easy to implement. After I explain them in this chapter, most of the rest of the book will focus on ways to put them to work in your classroom.

These conditions are so much a part of what should go on in a Quality School that I suggest they be posted on the wall of each classroom. For young students they would have to be written in simple language, but this should pose no problem. As soon as you post them, begin to explain them to your students. Even though in the beginning they may not understand much of what you are explaining, keep it brief and tell them not to worry. Tell them that these conditions are an important part of what makes this a new kind of school, that it will take time to understand them but there is no hurry. All you are trying to accomplish in the beginning is to sow the seeds of the ideas.

If they lose interest, do not labor over your explanation. Just make sure they perceive you believe that what you are trying to explain is very important. Keep in mind that what you are going to do with your students in a Quality School will be new to almost all of them. Many will resist as a matter of habit. Even if something sounds good, they will be wary both of it and of you. Accept that it will take them a while to understand that what you are now doing will improve the quality of their lives. Be patient; new ideas take hold slowly.

These same conditions should be posted in the school office so that anyone visiting the school, especially parents, can see what they are. It should be the goal of the staff to make an effort to understand the conditions well enough to answer questions that anyone who reads them might ask.

THE SIX CONDITIONS OF QUALITY SCHOOLWORK

1. There must be a warm, supportive classroom environment.

Quality Schoolwork (and the quality life that results from it) can only be achieved in a warm, supportive classroom environment. It cannot exist if there is an adversarial relationship between those who teach and those who are asked to learn. Not only need there be a strong, friendly feeling between teacher and students, this same feeling is necessary among the students, teachers, and administrators. Above all, there must be trust: They must all believe that the others have their welfare in mind. Without this trust, neither students nor teachers will make the effort needed to do quality work. Because the ability to talk to others who listen is the foundation of warmth and trust, the students must be encouraged to talk honestly and easily to their teacher and he or she to them. Under no circumstances should anyone in a Quality School attempt to coerce another person.

2. Students should be asked to do only useful work.

Quality work is always useful work; no student should be asked to do anything that does not make sense, such as to memorize material that will soon be forgotten because there is no use for it except in school. The Quality School teacher accepts that it is his or her professional responsibility to explain what is useful about everything he or she asks students to learn. Because they trust that their teachers will do this as soon as they can, students will be willing to do a substantial amount of work before its usefulness is clear to them. What they are asked to do need not be of immediate practical use, but it has to have some use: aesthetic, artistic, intellectual, or social.

If the real world requires that they learn useless material, such as much that is necessary to pass machine-scored, state assessment tests or college entrance tests, it should be explained to students that this has to be done so that their school can get state support or to help them to get into college. This is real-world nonsense: Nevertheless, Quality School teachers need to help them learn this material.

3. **Students are always asked to do the best they can do.**

Quality work requires time and effort, which means that in a Quality School students are given the time to make the necessary effort. They are told by their teacher that what is wanted in this class is always the best they can do at the time. As this is in sharp contrast to the experience of almost all students, it will take great patience on your part to get the process started. You are dealing with students most of whom have never thought of trying to do the best they can in an academic class. They are used to covering ground, not learning, and have never expended the effort to do quality work.

4. **Students are asked to evaluate their own work and improve it.**

Quality work, good as it may be, is never static. As Deming says, quality can almost always be improved. The Quality School teacher will make the effort to teach students how to evaluate their own work and then ask them to do this almost all of the time. (Of all that you do, this will be the most difficult to implement, for reasons that will be explained when self-evaluation is covered in detail later in this book.) Teachers in a Quality School would not nag, but they would send out a constant message that almost all work can be improved. Even if the initial work was judged as quality, students should be encouraged to see if a little additional effort would result in improvement. As stated, the school should stress that quality takes precedence over quantity. A large volume of low-quality work has nothing to do with education or, for that matter, anything of value.

5. **Quality work always feels good.**

Quality work always feels good for everyone involved, and it is tragic that so few students feel good in their academic classes now. Not only do students feel good as they succeed in doing what they judge is quality, but their teachers and parents also feel good as they observe the process. While it also feels good to be given or to purchase quality, it never feels as good as when it is personally achieved through hard work. In fact, there is no better human feeling than that which comes from the satisfaction of doing something useful that you believe is the very best you can do and finding that others agree. It is this good feeling (from need-satisfaction) that is the physiologic incentive to pursue the quality that is the goal of the Quality School.

6. **Quality work is never destructive.**

Quality is never achieved through doing anything destructive. Therefore, it is not quality to achieve good feelings through the use of addictive drugs or to harm people, most living creatures, property, or the environment, which belongs to all of us.

By the time they get past the first few grades in a traditional school, students are already skeptical of the value of school. It no longer feels as good as it did in kindergarten, and, as they have moved up from grade to grade, for the majority of students, there is less and less good feeling associated with learning. They also begin to hear a lot of bad things about what is coming, so they are pretty sure things are not going to get better.

25

As this happens, they do not look at teachers as being on their side. The fact that some teachers are on their side does not often help, because it makes what they are going through even more disappointing. They ask themselves, "If some teachers are on our side, why not more?" As early as the second or third grade, some students do not believe that you have their welfare in mind. They see you as their adversary, and the number who do not trust you grows as they move into middle school, where it levels off; by mid-high school, however, the number drops. By this time it is not so much that they now trust you, although many now do, but, confident they will graduate, students find school much less threatening.

Your first task in a Quality School is to persuade all your students to trust you. They must believe that, in all you ask them to do as well as in how you ask them to do it, you are on their side. Trust alone will rarely lead to Quality Schoolwork. You can count on this happening only if you implement the six conditions. What will help you to realize how important these conditions are is the way you will be treated if you teach in a Quality School. When you are treated as a professional and supervised according to these same conditions, the quality of your professional life will get better and better, and you will appreciate how important it is that your students have the same experience.

All this will take time. In the beginning, your students don't even know what quality is, much less that it is what they want. But **you know it.** You also know that, if you can implement these six conditions in your classroom, your students will feel good and will want to keep learning so that they continue to feel good. As they do, and as you teach them control theory, they will become aware that quality is what they want and that, in your class, they can achieve it.

CHAPTER FOUR

Your Students Need to Know You and Like You

If you accept that the goal of a Quality School is that all students will do some Quality Schoolwork, you also have to accept that it will be up to you to persuade them to work much harder than they do now. As you well know, this is going to be difficult, because most students are not used to working hard in school or anywhere else. The few who do work hard do so much more to please their parents, or someone they love at home, than to please their teachers.

We also know that the traditional way to get students to work hard, boss-management, does not work. Even when we get parents involved, for the most part it is to get them to boss their children far more than to lead them, so this option has been generally unsuccessful. Therefore, if we can't depend on reward and punishment whether teachers or parents do it, we are left with no other option than to do something that is different from what we are doing now, which is **to implement the six conditions of quality in our classrooms.** In this chapter, I want to focus on the first condition, creating a warm and supportive climate in the classroom.

As much as I have generally explained how to do this, there is one specific aspect of creating this climate that I have yet to explain. This is **to teach so that your students get to know you far better than most do now.** When anyone works hard for another person, and almost all students in school work for a teacher who is their manager, the amount of effort they put out depends to a great extent on:

1. How well they know the person they are working for.

2. How much they like what they know.

If there is an axiom to lead-management, it is **"the better we know someone and the more we like about what we know, the harder we will work for that person."** Control theory explains that we will work hard for those we care for (**belonging**), for those we respect and who respect us (**power**), for those with whom we laugh (**fun**), for those who allow us to think and act for ourselves (**freedom**), and for those who help us to make our lives secure (**survival**). The more that all five of these needs are satisfied in our relationship with the manager who asks us to do the work, the harder we will work for that manager.

Acting on this knowledge, teachers in a Quality

School will make an effort to do as much as possible to help their students know them. The following is a list of what I suggest you do to accomplish this. I realize the list is specific, but suggestions have to be specific or they are meaningless. I do not expect you to do exactly as I say. Feel free to do as you think best. What I suggest here, as in the rest of this book, I hope will be taken as a guide. To me, you are all professional teachers; there are no commands in this book.

Also, take your time, do only as much as you are comfortable with, and keep in mind that my suggestions are directed more to what to do than to how you should do it. The reason to go slowly is that if you try too hard or go too fast, your students may interpret what you are doing as overselling and may doubt your sincerity. Also, because they are not used to this approach, they may interpret too much effort on your part as coercive, and you will be less effective. It is also best if you integrate these suggestions into the give-and-take of your teaching. Occasions will arise when covering this or that point on the list will be natural and easy, and you should strive to take advantage of these occasions.

What I will suggest may seem to you to be excessive. Partly, this may be because very few people who have taught or managed you have ever done anything close to what I am asking here. But some have, and I believe that these are the teachers you worked the hardest for and whom you still remember. This certainly was the case for me. If you take your time, you will find it is very enjoyable to implement these suggestions. In a

Quality School, it is important that you enjoy what you do. As your students get to know you, they will, in turn, reveal more and more about themselves. **As they do, you and they will gain much of the closeness that is needed if you are to satisfy the first condition of quality.**

During the first few months you are with your students, look for natural occasions to tell them:

1. Who you are.

2. What you stand for.

3. What you will ask them to do.

4. What you will not ask them to do.

5. What you will do for them.

6. What you will not do for them.

Let me now go through this list item by item and explain why I think each point is important. Do not, however, restrict yourself to this list. Add anything you believe will increase what you and your students know and like about each other.

Who You Are
Because people satisfy our needs, we are all very curious about each other. One thing we like so much

about television is that we get to see and hear people in ways that would otherwise be impossible. If these are famous people, good or bad, we cannot know too much about their lives. But television rarely shows people we know personally: If someone we know is on, we make an extra effort to see that program. Suppose that your school principal was scheduled to be on television. Wouldn't you make every effort to hear what she had to say? Further, suppose she revealed something about her life that you did not suspect—that as a fifteen-year-old she had been in a lot of trouble and had been sent to a reform school, where she got help and turned her life around?

Wouldn't your relationship with her change to some extent—most likely for the better? Might you not respect her a little more for having overcome early adversity and listen to her more attentively when she advised you on how to deal with a problem student? Wouldn't she become a little more human to you than before? Remember that, as an adult, you are much more acquainted than children with the ways of people. Still, as sophisticated as you may be, you appreciated learning things you didn't know about a person as important to you as your principal.

Children are not sophisticated. Most of them don't know very much about the people they live with, much less anyone else. Even to those in the upper grades, who their teachers are is, for the most part, a complete mystery. Not knowing, they fantasize and may build a false image of you based on very little real knowledge. We all remember doing this as students. When, in some unusual school situation, such as an extended out-of-town field trip, we got to know a lot more about a teacher, we often changed our opinion completely, usually for the better. As are all people, students are hungry to know about the people who tell them what to do. Yet most of them remain in the dark.

Your students are interested in statistics such as your age, your marital status, whether or not you have children and, if so, their ages. Do you have a mother, father, or grandparent in your life? Do you live in a house or an apartment? What kind of car do you drive? Even more, they want to know about your interests: What you have done besides teach, what your favorite television programs are, what music you listen to, what food you like best and what food you dislike. The list could go on and on, but if you do not make your stories too long, they will be fascinated with what seems so unimportant to you.

What You Stand For

Most interesting to all of us, and usually totally unknown to your students about you, is what people stand for. Do you practice what you preach, and, if you don't, why not? For example, what do you do when your children misbehave or don't do their homework or don't clean up their room? Do you read books; what are they; will you bring one you especially like to class, read some excerpts, and explain why what you read is so important to you?

Do you have a stand on what's going on in the world—for example, on the riots in our cities—and what would you do about them if you had a chance to do something? Do you disagree with your parents or with your husband or wife, and what do you do when you disagree? Do you vote, and what do you do to find out who to vote for? Do you think grades are important, and, if not, what is more important in school?

Again, the list could go on, but what you stand for and why you stand for it is of endless interest to your students. It is from people like you, who, in a Quality School, they would respect very much, that they begin to form their own opinions. Not knowing any responsible adult well, too many students form opinions in a vacuum of noninformation or information from biased or ill-informed people. To form their own opinions, they need to find out what people like you think about and why. Feel free also not to divulge what you stand for if it is personal and uncomfortable to share or is markedly different from the standards of the community you teach in. Students, however, should be taught how to state an unpopular opinion and defend it. If you can do this, they will have learned a great deal from you that they may not be able to learn from anyone else.

You also might want to model your unpopular stand rather than express it. For example, suppose you don't believe in killing anything or anyone, which would make you against the death penalty in what you know is a meat-eating, eye-for-an-eye, tooth-for-a-tooth community. You explain that you do not eat meat and, when asked why, explain that you are against killing higher organisms like animals, and that you believe you can live a good life on vegetables and milk products. If pushed on the death penalty, you might say you are against all killing of higher organisms, including people. But you would not say that your opinion is the only one; there are other acceptable opinions, but this is what you believe.

If students push you to teach them how to find out what to believe, you would say that there is no sure way, but there are accepted ways that work for many people, like turning to their parents, to their ministers, or to the works of great men and women like those they study in school. In the end it is up to each individual to figure this out for him- or herself, and that is how you are going to teach your class, because this is how you live your life.

Finally, if I were you (this is my belief, and I would hope all teachers in a Quality School would share it), I would explain to the class, and reexplain as the situation arises, as it often will, that most of all you believe that no one should put another person down. (As I will cover later in the book when I discuss evaluation, Deming believes that no human being should ever publicly evaluate another human being.) Explain that most of the trouble and friction among people, in or out of school, is caused by putting others down. Schools are filled with both student and faculty cliques and groups based on power, or lack of it, that cause endless friction and make it impossible for quality work to flourish. Quality is achieved through harmony and respect; there is no other way.

What You Will Ask Them to Do

In a Quality School, you should make sure that they know what you will ask them to do: Never surprise your students. Much of this will be described in detail in the next chapter and has been covered to some extent in *The Quality School.* Here I would like to summarize and also to explain how best to tell this to your class. First of all, telling them what you will ask them to do is meaningless if you don't, yourself, do as you ask them to do. For example, if you ask them to be in class on time ready to go to work, then you must be in class on time ready to go to work. If you tell them that this material is going or not going to be on a test, then it must be or not be on the test: no exceptions.

In a Quality School, although you will not punish or put anyone down, you should tell them that this does not mean you will not handle problems. Tell them that you are going to ask them to work with you to solve any problem that arises, no matter how small. You will ask them to do this as individuals, in small groups, or as a whole class. You are much more interested in them solving their own problems than in you doing it for them. You also should tell your students that the purpose of school is to teach them how to use what they have learned, and that you will expect them to be able to show you they are able to do this. Exactly how to do this is extensively explained in material I have already written, but, because it is so important, it will be covered further in this book.

What You Will Not Ask Them to Do

Considering that most of your students will come from traditional schools, as soon as a change is in place, tell your students what it is and that you will no longer ask them to do what you asked them to do before. This will help them to see that you are different from the teachers they are used to. For example, when you are sure you are ready, explain clearly and specifically that there are no threats, punishments, or busywork in a Quality School and that you will not ask them to learn anything that is not useful.

In general, as you read this book, you will find there are many things that are routine in a traditional school that are not part of a Quality School and, as you get used to **not** doing these things, tell your students what they are. More and more, they will both learn and appreciate the difference between this school and the schools they previously attended. They will trust you more, and your credibility will increase.

What You Will Do for Them

As long as they come to class, you will help them in any way you can or, if possible, in any way they want. You are their friend, you are always on their side, it will never be you against them. For example, if they need more time to figure something out or to do a better job, you will give it to them or advise them to do it at home or in the library. If they have questions, you will either answer them or find someone who can. If they have an idea about how to make things better, no matter if it is in class or anyplace else in their lives, if you have time, you will listen to them. You will make it your business to try to have the time, but they may have to help you by working quietly while you work with a few students at a time to do this.

If they have any problem in their lives, you will try to help, but most of what you help them with will be limited to school. I suggest you tell them that at specific hours on specific days, you are available at home to talk to them or their parents on the phone. If you and they are on good terms, they will not abuse this privilege.

You will conduct class meetings whenever they think there is anything that needs discussing and encourage them to speak out. You are there to help and support, never to boss. You will also explain that you will never threaten, punish, or put down anyone at any time. At the same time, tell them that you are not perfect. If they find you are not doing as you say, they should not be afraid to tell you, and you will explain or change. As you do this, don't be afraid to tell them that when problems of any kind arise, you will need their help. They should not be afraid to offer it. You will not think they are out of line when they offer the help you need, and, even if you are in a bad mood, while you may growl a little, you will never punish them. Although there is no punishment in your classes, problems must be solved.

You also want your students to know that you will be in touch with their parents or guardians to tell them or show them what you are doing in class that is leading to the quality work their children are now doing. Further, with the help of parents, whose support you need, you might want to plan ways in which your students can take what they have learned in your class out to the community and use it. Go out into the community to learn. Visit a court that is in session, and ask the judge to spend a little time explaining the court system to them.

What you want their parents to know is that you believe that learning is a lot more than listening to a lecture, reading a book, taking a test, or doing a lot of useless compulsory homework. With their help and cooperation, you are open to anything that you believe will lead to quality work. There is nothing useful and sensible that you won't try to do with your students to teach them that what they learn in school is useful in their lives.

What You Will Not Do for Them

You will not do their work or figure out their problems for them. You will not tell them what to do if you believe it is something that they could figure out for themselves. You will spend a lot of time teaching them how to evaluate their own work. Once they know how to do this, you will expect them to do it and to defend their evaluation of their work against you or anyone else. Almost all your students will have come from an educational environment where they always turned to the teacher to tell them how they were doing: This is what you want to change. If they ask for your opinion, give it, but not unless they are also willing to express their opinions and to defend them. Explain that to be successful in life, we must evaluate ourselves and work to improve: We cannot and should not depend on others to do this for us.

I believe that what I have suggested here will help them to know you and trust you. As you try to do as I suggest, you will discover that there is much more you can do to help you and your students to get to know each other than is suggested here. You will also find that there is much that you can do that is nonverbal, such as a pat on the back, a gesture, or a supportive expression on your face. The main point of what I am suggesting is that anything you do that helps them to know you and to know that **you stand for them doing Quality School-work** is worth trying to do. Your goal is that they know you well enough **and like what they know about you enough so that they see you as the best person they have ever met besides their families.** They should think of you a lot and carry your picture front and center in their quality worlds for the rest of their lives. You should not settle for less.

CHAPTER FIVE

Quality School Teachers Teach Useful Skills

When you work for a living, you can almost always see the usefulness of what you are asked to do, whether it is making a product or performing a service that customers want. If on a rare occasion you are asked to do something that no one is interested in, such as I did day after day in an army laboratory, you quickly become uncomfortable. What causes your discomfort is that your basic need for power is being frustrated: There is no power in doing something useless.

Jobs, however, are rarely completely useless. More often, some jobs are seen as more useful than others, or, put in another way, some jobs lead to much higher quality products or services than others. Therefore, what we are talking about in the world of business is more than usefulness, it is quality. The higher the quality at a competitive price, the more successful the organization that achieves it and the more secure its employees. For

workers, however, especially in well-managed businesses, the incentive to work hard and do quality work
is more than job security, **it is the joy of being associated with quality products and quality people.**

Traditional schools provide no such incentive.
Teachers are secure in their jobs even if many of their
students do not learn very much, but there is little joy in
teaching in such schools. It is the same for students.
Although they are secure as long as they do enough
work to get by, few ever do enough to experience the
joy of quality work. Without this good feeling, they
have little incentive to do much more than most do now.

For Deming, how students and teachers feel is very
important. He says, "A system of schools … should be a
component in a system of education in which pupils
from toddlers on up **take joy in learning,** free from the
fear of grades and gold stars, and in which teachers take
joy in their work, free from fear of ranking. It would be
a system that recognizes differences between pupils and
differences between teachers."[5]

That students should enjoy academic work is not a
concern of traditional schools. It is perfectly acceptable
to try to coerce students into doing totally joyless work,
such as memorizing material that both they and their
teachers know they will forget a few days after the test.
This is the school equivalent of digging holes and then
filling them in, a traditional punishment in the boss-
managed army of my time, where the motto was: Do
what we tell you whether you see it as useful or not! In
school, unlike the army, where just the troublemakers

are punished, all students are asked to do a lot of useless work and punished if they balk.

A major flaw in our traditional educational system is that we try but consistently fail to "motivate" students to do useless work. Boss-managers can't seem to learn that there is no way to motivate people to do what has no chance of satisfying their needs. Turned off by the pain of doing so much useless work, some students even refuse to learn useful skills like writing and math.

Therefore, following the **second** condition of quality, it is always **useful,** and the **fifth** condition, it is always **joyful, neither teachers nor students in Quality Schools would ever be asked to do anything useless.** If there is any doubt in your mind or in your students' minds about the usefulness of what you and they are asked to do, both you and they would be encouraged to express this doubt. As soon as possible, your principal should explain its usefulness to you, and you should do the same for your students. All teachers (and administrators) would know enough control theory to know that only useful work can provide the incentive students need to expend the effort to do quality work. Quality work, the goal of a Quality School, is then able to provide its own powerful incentive: It is joyful.

In a Quality School, your job is to take the time to **explain to your students the usefulness of what you ask them to do.** As easy as this is to say, initially you will find it difficult to do. This is not because you don't want to do it, but because it will be new to many of you. Very few teachers (if any) did it for you when you were a K-12 student. As a professional teacher in a traditional school, you may have recognized the value of doing this and may do it, but, unlike a Quality School, the school you teach in has **never asked you to do it.** When you accept the assignment of teaching in a Quality School, you also accept that you will be expected to explain the usefulness of all you ask your students to learn. This chapter is to help you to do this and to reassure you that doing it is not as difficult as you may fear.

SKILLS VERSUS INFORMATION

When we talk about usefulness, we have to distinguish between teaching life skills, which are almost always useful, and teaching information, which is only useful if the students see its value or you can convince them that committing it to memory has value. **The difference between the skills I am talking about and information is clear: skills are what you use, information is what you know.** For example, writing is a **skill** that students will use for the rest of their lives. Recognizing the flag of Nepal is **information** that, occasionally, a few students may use. To attempt to teach things like this to all students is senseless.

The usual rationale for memorizing information is that it helps people to do whatever they want to do as they live their lives. But, unless this information is strongly tied to the skill of using it, this is rarely the case. For example, while knowing the parts of a cell may be very valuable to a practicing cellular biologist, memorizing this same information is painful for all but a handful of the millions of students who are tested for this each year in high school. Instead of their getting interested in biology, they turn off, a common result of this senseless way to teach. This is not to say that you should not teach students basic cellular biology, but you can teach a lot of usable biology without asking any student to memorize anything.

It is now popular to try to force students to become culturally literate, and books are written on what students should know. But a Quality School teacher would not try to "make" her students culturally literate by asking them to memorize a lot of information. Rather, she would use discussion, reading, and noncompulsory "talk it over with your family" homework assignments to acquaint them with the value of knowing what is good to know about our culture. There is a good chance that they will remember what is good to know; there is little chance that they will remember what you try to make them memorize.

Students, however, are not only asked to learn useless information. They are pressured to learn it through the threat of punishment and are severely punished with low or failing grades if they refuse to make the effort to memorize what to them is useless. This is a high price to pay for retaining the destructive tradition that for centuries has made memorizing an important component of education. It may have been important before Gutenberg, but not since then.

In a Quality School, no attempt would be made to

force students to memorize. Not only does this not add quality to their lives, it persuades many students to dislike school. Quality Schools will focus on basic skills. They are called **basic** because most students know enough about them to want to learn them. **To almost all students, it is self-evident that the basic skills of speaking, reading, writing, calculating, and problem solving are well worth learning**. These life skills are to getting along well in the world as food and shelter are to staying alive.

In a Quality School, information will not be taught unless it falls into one or more of the following four categories, all understandable and almost always acceptable both to teachers and to students. In the order of their importance, these categories are the following:

1. **Information directly related to a life skill.**

   For example, students should be exposed to the fact that grammar is an important component of writing and speaking as they learn these skills, to the fact that the times tables may help them calculate as they learn the skill of mathematical problem solving, and that directions like north and south are important to the skills of map reading. This information need not be memorized by rote. It will be assimilated as the skill is used, and, in a Quality School, the skills that are taught will be used a great deal. No matter how much a student is threatened, information that he or she does not use will not be retained.

2. **Information that students express a desire to learn.**

If, in the frequent teacher-student discussions that are held in a Quality School, the students express a desire to learn some particular information, teachers should do their best to teach it or to help students find where to look it up.

3. **Information that the teacher believes is especially useful.**

For example, if you believe it is useful to learn about William Shakespeare and his writing, teach it. If you strongly believe that memorizing some information has great value, even if, initially, it is foreign to your students, it is likely that you will be able to communicate this belief to your students and they will want to learn it. Conversely, you would not try to teach (or as a professional be forced to teach) what you do not believe is worth making the effort to learn.

4. **Information required for college.**

Information such as dates in history or rivers in geography may be of little educational use, but it may be required for college entrance exams. In a Quality School, the teacher will discuss this honestly with the students, and together they will decide on how much effort should be expended to learn what is useless except as it might be a ticket to college.

49

TEACHING SKILLS

In the remainder of this chapter I will focus on how best to teach the five life skills in a Quality Elementary School. They would be the core of the curriculum because they are the foundation of all education. I don't want to imply that the teaching of these basic skills is all that should be taught, or that it should be restricted to the elementary school; but this is the natural place to start. In the next chapter I will expand this explanation to the teaching of both skills and information in the secondary school.

Ask elementary students if they want to learn to read, write, calculate, and speak well by the time they leave for middle school, and almost all will answer yes. Then ask if they want to be able to enjoy reading a newspaper, write a good letter, calculate well enough to solve everyday problems like those that arise when playing games like Monopoly, and speak well enough to interview successfully for a job. They will again say yes. To teach this much to students who want to learn it is where we would start in a Quality Elementary School. Our goal, however, would be for all students to be able to demonstrate that they can use these skills to do some quality work.

Reading

As the professional teacher, it is up to you to figure out what your students should read. For example, how much should you use the textbooks? While you should use any material that you believe has value, I suggest that the emphasis should be on reading books. Eventually, as part of teaching them to speak competently, you would discuss with them what they want to read, but, in the beginning, you should provide them with useful material to read and, in the primary grades, teach them to read it. To get them interested in learning how and then continuing to read, research shows that there is no better way than reading to them. It could be as much as an hour a day, but how much and how much at one time would be up to you.

To emphasize the importance of books, teachers in a Quality Elementary School might, with the help of the students, build libraries in their classrooms. When students have easy access to their own libraries, books take on a value that cannot be acquired in any other way. To find the books for these libraries, people in the community that have suitable books gathering dust should be canvassed and asked to contribute them. Canvassing a neighborhood populated by older people whose children are gone from the home is a good source of these books. Your students, aided by their parents, should be taught how to ask for books for their libraries, a good exercise in the skill of effective communication and selling oneself.

Books could be donated or loaned, and a receipt with a promise to return them at the end of the school year would be made up in the class and provided to lenders when desired. The students should use this project to learn that giving and loaning are common ways to solve problems when money is short. If possible, enlist the aid of a local newspaper, radio, or television station to publicize your effort. With the help of your students, make signs that you can post in the neighborhood to announce the fact that on a certain weekend day, you and your class (your students would have the job of enlisting their parents to help) would be canvassing the neighborhood for books.

If they were gifts, as most would be, you could give the donors a receipt to deduct the donation from their income tax and use this process to teach students about taxes and the tax benefits of charity. If the books were a loan, you would keep these books on a separate shelf marked with the owner's name. Even with small children, you would appoint a librarian or succession of librarians who would learn the useful skill of keeping track of the books. To teach children speaking skills, encourage them to give oral book reports or try to sell others on a book they liked a lot. You should make a big deal out of your library: It would introduce them to the real world of libraries. It will be easier to interest them in what are now their own books than in what they don't own, such as the textbooks or books from the school library.

One suggestion that could create a lot of excitement would be to invite local authors, who might then donate one of their books to your library, to come and talk to the class about writing. Most authors are anxious to do something like this, and some are accessible. You might involve the local public access channel on cable television to make a half hour available to your school to have children discuss the books that are in their classroom libraries. Seeing their friends on television would have a good chance of getting children's attention, and this would create more interest in reading books. The class-room libraries could each be branches of the school library, and, as faculty, you would encourage students from every class to visit each other's libraries. All this should be coordinated by student librarians.

A classroom library that the students helped to put together would provide them with the valuable experi-ence of ownership. In a traditional school, it does not even cross children's minds that they own anything; to them everything is owned by the staff and the school. We all know that what we don't own and what we have no control over acquiring has much less chance to be seen by any of us as quality than something that is ours. In a Quality School, the goal would be to tell students that this is their school and involve them in as many decisions about school as you can. The classroom library is an example of a wonderful way to get this learning process started.

I want to reemphasize that I make this and all other suggestions not so much for you to follow exactly, but to give you an example of the kind of useful things that you would be encouraged to figure out for yourself in a Quality School. As you get the idea of concentrating on teaching useful skills, you will think of many other ways to get your students usefully involved with books and reading.

Writing

When I talk about writing, I mean writing something that is worth reading. I don't mean the skill of jotting down a grocery list, which, of course, should be taught but is not really writing in the sense I am discussing writing here. Because it is so much easier than writing by hand, I strongly recommend that writing in a Quality School should mostly be word processing on computers. Besides having a school computer room, each class should have at least one computer, so students can be made familiar with the machine that has rendered all other ways to write obsolete. Nothing turns students off more than to know that what they are being taught is out of date. Whether you like it or not, for serious writing— and in a Quality School nothing is more serious than writing—pens and pencils are outmoded.

From the first grade, children would be taught simple word processing and encouraged to write. If enough computers are not available in the school, you might work out a plan with parents and grandparents to canvass their neighborhood to find out who has a computer that he or she would let your students use, and who might be willing to teach a child to write on it. If needed, businesses with computers that are not in use at night would be asked if, under adult supervision, one or two nights a week, a few of these computers can be used for writing. There would be no higher priority than figuring out how to get enough access to computers to take care of the needs of your students.

Students would be encouraged to write anything that

interested them and to write a lot. Letters, plays, stories, an autobiography, even a book, all would be taught as worth writing. It would be up to the professional teacher to figure out how to interest them in writing different things, but, on a computer, getting them started will turn out to be less of a problem than stopping them once they start. As almost all tests in a Quality School would be written, the students would want to write well. Access to computers to write tests (the computer room could be reserved for test taking) would give them this chance.

Since the goal of a Quality School is quality work, and since improving what we write is so easy on a computer, I don't see how we can have Quality Schoolwork without giving students access to computers. While computers can be used for many other purposes besides writing, this is by far the most necessary of their many uses. To help all students to learn to write and to use computers in other ways, students who had computer expertise (many students do in most schools, some more than their teachers) would be recruited to teach their skills to other students. Parents, adult volunteers, high school students with expertise, a cadre of volunteer experts could be recruited by the staff of the school and called upon as needed.

Calculating and Math

Calculating in a Quality School would be easy to teach and easy to learn. Students like to calculate because they like the experience of solving problems for which there is a right answer. What they don't like is not knowing how to do a problem, or being put down for getting a wrong answer, as we do too often when we test calculating in a traditional school. In a Quality School, as spelled out clearly in the previous chapter, students would know they are here to learn, learning is never connected to time, students are never put down, and the staff believes all students can learn.

Nowhere is the value of teaching this way more apparent than in teaching first calculation and then math. The many intelligent adults we meet constantly who lack confidence in their ability to do simple calculations are all products of the traditional system that jammed math down their throats and punished them when they choked on it. As will be explained in detail in later chapters, students in small groups should be given problems to do and told that, if they need help, to ask for it first from the students in their group, then from student teaching assistants, and finally from teachers. (The recruiting and training of student tutors and teaching assistants will be described in a later chapter.)

Elementary school students should learn the major calculation operations of addition, subtraction, multiplication, division, decimals, percentages, and fractions. Only commonly used fractions—halves through tenths, and then twelfths and sixteenths—would be taught and tested for. All other fractions would be handled with decimals and percentages. Students who wanted to learn more complex fractions would be encouraged to do so, but it would not be a useful requirement of a Quality

School. The above calculations, learned in elementary school, are sufficient for the large majority of us who do not need advanced mathematics like algebra. However, math from algebra on would be a major part of the curriculum of any post-elementary Quality School.

Students would be started in calculating early and told that they cannot fail. As in all subjects eventually, but immediately in calculation and math, there would be no compulsory homework or written tests. As soon as any student in the small working group believes that he has mastered a calculating procedure, he would raise his hand and then both show and tell his teacher or any designated math helper (student or volunteer), in step-by-step stages, how he can work a typical problem that is an example of the procedure he has mastered. As soon as one procedure is mastered he goes on to the next. With enough time to learn, with no reason even to want to cheat, with the opportunity to explain what they did to an encouraging, patient teacher or tutor, all students would learn to calculate well.

From calculation, students would go on to math, which, in this early stage, would not be algebra or traditional mathematics. It would be the ability to solve real-life problems using the ability to calculate. The advanced or formal math like algebra could wait until they knew all the calculation processes, or it could be integrated into each calculation process. It would be up to the teacher to choose which way is best or to figure out a better way. What I suggest here, while proven, is only a suggestion. I am sure that many teachers will figure out ways to teach this subject that are as good as or better than these suggestions.

The math I am talking about is traditionally called story problems. Research shows that we teach the ability to calculate quite well to many students. But these same students do not know how to use this ability to solve real problems, such as how much paint to buy to paint a room of certain dimensions, or how much wood to buy to build a bookshelf that will hold five hundred average-size books. In fact, if the class has a library, calculating how to make the bookshelves for the books is a good example of a real-world problem. In a Quality School, to give students the sense of ownership, the students should be taught how the school is financed and asked to calculate how much money is needed to pay the teachers, heat the building, etc., all of which requires simple math.

Math textbooks should be considered to help teach calculation and simple math. There are many good elementary math books. The problem now is that good books are badly used. Besides the math problems taken from these books, **people in the community should be asked to submit math problems that an elementary student should know how to solve.** If this were done, the community could not complain that students aren't learning what they need to learn in school. Concerned members of the community could meet and tell the teachers specifically what they think is needed in arithmetic problem solving. Then, if you agree, you would teach it until the students could **demonstrate** to anyone in the community that they know what they should. (How to evaluate what students actually know in Quality Schools will be covered in a later chapter.)

Speaking

Helping students to learn to speak convincingly and grammatically is the skill that has the highest payoff in the real world. The best way to accomplish this is to spend a lot of time talking with your students as they work individually or in small groups. As they talk, and as you encourage them to keep talking, they will naturally try to improve the way they express themselves. As they do, you may want at times to point out places where they can improve their grammar. As you do this, try to explain that the purpose of learning grammar is to improve the clarity of what they are trying to say. Students tend not to understand this and view grammar as a chore if it is taught separate from its use.

The best way to get them interested in talking is to convince them, by showing interest, that you want to hear what they have to say. Along with this, run a lot of class meetings, talk over all problems, and try to solve them. Use the meetings to make plans and try to involve all the students in these discussions. Don't be afraid to gently confront the nontalkers and ask for their opinion. Say things like, "John, you haven't said anything for a while, and I want your opinion." He may not talk then, but if you keep looking at him, he'll begin to get the idea you really want to hear what he has to say, and he'll speak up.

Beyond what you do in class, try to involve your students in projects in which they have to talk to the community. As stated, the collection of books for the class library would be an ideal way to do this. This is salespersonship, and it is an important skill that can best be taught through simulation in class. Have a student act as a homeowner (or renter), and then have other students make a pitch for books. You might bring in a parent or you could play the person in the home. Do this in small groups, and wait until they get pretty good before sending them out. Explain to them that what they are selling is themselves. If they can come across as competent, caring students, they will get plenty of books.

Problem Solving

While math, which is the goal of learning to calculate, is obviously a common form of problem solving, you should also introduce them early to the skill of solving real-life problems. Teach them that the core of problem solving is to learn to use information in a logical way and that the only real purpose of gathering information is to use it. It is usually better to use current community problems than to make up problems or take them from a book, but any problem that interests your students is a good problem.

Here in Los Angeles we usually have a shortage of

water, and recently the whole community was asked to get involved in conserving water. A problem like this could be used to teach basic problem solving skills and get students used to the idea that they could contribute something to solving community problems. For example, students could be taught how to conserve water and to begin to practice what they have learned in school. They could be taught to read the school water meter and use these readings to check out which methods seem to save the most water. They could learn charting and graphing to illustrate what they are learning, and a computer person could be recruited to teach them how to set this up and graph it in a variety of ways on a computer. From this they could use their own house or apartment to do the same thing, reading the meter and charting. Discussions and debates could be held to argue differences in opinions, and experts could be brought in to give their ideas on conservation.

Students could also be prepared to make house calls, explain to people what they have learned in school, and teach them how to use these water saving methods at home. This would help them to use their ability to speak as well as to solve problems. This is only one of the many ways a Quality School teacher could get students involved using the skills learned in school in the real world. It would make education much more popular in the community and make the connection, not often made in our schools today, between what is learned in school and the real world.

CHAPTER SIX

Teaching Useful Information in the Secondary School

Many of us remember that, as students, especially after elementary school, we were asked to memorize a lot of information. In geography we memorized the states and their capitals, in science, rocks and planets, in biology, birds, digestive juices, and bacteria, in history, the places and dates of battles, and in social studies, sections of the constitution and the structure of our government. We memorized this information because someone, somewhere long ago had made a case for its usefulness that our school accepted. At the time we learned it, no one could make that case believable to us. For example, I can't remember any student ever saying, "Great, this stuff's so useful I am going to remember it for the rest of my life." If we had a good memory, it may have stuck with us for a while, but, eventually, almost all of it was forgotten.

Does information have to be retained to make the

effort to learn it worthwhile? I remember learning a lot that I do not remember today, but I also remember that, at the time I learned it, I thought it was worth thinking about and talking about in class, especially if I cared for the teacher. In one case that I especially remember, I loved the teacher. I did it for her. What I still remember about this experience today is not the long-forgotten information, **but that she taught me to love to learn.** That, not the specifics she taught, is what made my experience with her so valuable.

Quality School teachers will have to deal with people in the community who argue that to succeed in our culture we need to memorize a great many things that are common to the culture. In response to them, you should make the point that our culture changes so rapidly that it is hard to say what will and will not be of cultural value in the future. We cannot possibly know. When I mention Shangri-La in a talk today, I see a lot of puzzled young faces. In my youth that fictitious country was so well-known I never thought it would pass out of common knowledge, but it has. What is retained by a culture is what continues to be need-satisfying, but who is to know what information will continue to be so need-satisfying that it is worth trying to force students to learn it?

The best question to ask to determine what is need-satisfying is, "Can you use it in your life **now or in the foreseeable future.**" For example, when I read about or hear hard rock music, I am abysmally ignorant, but, as of yet, I have no desire to expend the effort to learn about what does not satisfy my needs. No one has ever tried to teach me its value, so I can't say that it could never satisfy my needs. If someone I respected could teach me how I could use it for enjoyment, I might make the effort to learn about it. The information we are asked to memorize must be useful now or in the foreseeable future, or we won't make the effort to learn it no matter how much we are coerced to do so.

In the last chapter I explained that in elementary school it is most important that students become proficient in the five basic academic skills and that any information taught be closely connected to these almost always usable skills. In a Quality Secondary School, every attempt should be made to continue the practice of connecting knowledge with the skill to use it. As a Quality Secondary School teacher, you will find it especially difficult, because you will have to be willing to make an even bigger break with tradition than if you taught in an elementary school, where teaching skills is more predominant. Except for well-taught physics, chemistry, and some, but not all, mathematics, the way biology, history, geography, government, foreign languages, and literature are taught and tested for requires students to memorize information much more than to learn the skill of using it.

For example, in geography, students now spend most of their time memorizing surface features, such as rivers, oceans, and mountains, and geologic formations, such as tectonic plates. They can get credit for the course, even get a good grade, if they can remember enough of this information to pass traditional, closed-book, objective tests. Even if traditional teachers attempt to teach how this information could be used in their students' lives, they tend to base their grades far more on their ability to remember than on whether they know how to use what they have been asked to memorize.

There is little concern that they retain this memorized material after the test is over. For example, before students take the SAT, almost all of them are busy rememorizing what they previously learned and then forgot. After the SAT, they will forget it even more quickly than the first time, a sad exercise in digging information holes and then filling them in a few days later. It is much easier for teachers to test or evaluate whether students can remember something than it is to figure out how to evaluate their ability to use the information. But as I explained in the last chapter, this way to teach and evaluate is so joyless that both students and teachers turn off and education grinds to a halt. You will have to work harder to teach and evaluate usefully, but the payoff in quality and in the joy of teaching should more than make up for the effort.

In a Quality Secondary School, **there will be no requirement to memorize anything. There will be total emphasis on teaching students how they can use information, like the parts of a cell, in their lives either now or later.** As stated, this is now done in well-taught math, physics, and chemistry courses, so it is not that I am suggesting something completely new. However, teachers of the "memory" courses, which make up a majority of what is taught in secondary schools, will have to learn to do something that most have never experienced, much less ever done. Even in your college education, most of you experienced neither useful teaching nor teachers who focused on usefulness, so it will be up to you to learn this on your own. It will take a lot of effort: Learning to teach and evaluate this way is, perhaps, the most difficult part of becoming a Quality Secondary School teacher.

The best way to teach a skill-based curriculum is to relate what you are trying to teach to the real world. For example, all of us, including students, are interested in some of the news of the day. It is called news because we can relate it to our lives. AIDS, or HIV, is almost always in the news. For the next few years, if you teach biology, you will not have to teach most of your students that Magic Johnson is infected with the HIV virus; they know it. Starting with this interesting information, you could take your students into almost every nook and cranny of medical biology by teaching them about AIDS. All this could be done without anyone memorizing anything except a very few basic facts that few would ever forget. For example, all students may not practice safe sex, but they will all remember what it is that they should do.

As you teach, **emphasize what interests you.** If you are interested in birds, focus on birds when you teach biology. If Poe is one of your favorite authors, teach his writings when you teach English. If the Reconstruction and the failure of blacks to win civil rights after the Civil War is one of your interests, teach that, and also teach that it represents a recurrence of much that is typical of history. If your students see you as a need-satisfying person, anything you are interested in will have a good chance of interesting them. We gain our interests mostly from picking up on the interests of people we care for and respect: **Don't worry about what you should teach as much as what you want to teach.** As long as they remember you, they will have learned information that you value as a professional and they will have profited from being in your classes.

Have respect for their interests. Talk to them and try to find out what interests them and then try to tailor your teaching to their interests. Do not be disappointed if they are not interested in anything that is a part of the "regular" curriculum, and don't be surprised if, when you ask them what interests them, they express no interest in anything: They may just look blank.

By the time they get to high school in a traditional school system, most students are so resigned to adults paying no attention to their interests that they can't immediately relate to your asking what interests them. You may have to guess or stick to an interest of your own until they begin to catch on that things are different in this school: You really are interested in what they want to know. You need to be patient and persistent. They are skeptical of adults who claim to be interested in them, and this skepticism takes a long time to wear off. In time, however, they will begin to express their interests and then, if you can teach them more about what they want to know, you will capture their interest. When you do, their interest in all that you teach will be enhanced.

If you are a staff member discussing this chapter in a school that is a long way from making the commitment to become a Quality School, I can hear you saying to each other, "This guy's crazy. There is no school in the world that would let us get away with what he suggests here." I'm not crazy, but you are right, there are almost no schools where teachers feel free to do as I suggest. This is because there are very few Quality Schools, just as there are few quality factories or quality services in this country.

Quality depends on leadership. Most workers and lower-level managers, like teachers, are used to being bossed. I wish there were a lot of precedents I could point to, but there are not. You, who are attempting to become Quality teachers in committed Quality Schools, will be the precedents. Your administrators are encouraging you to change to the new system. My advice is, "Take advantage of this opportunity. If you don't, you may never get another chance."

CHAPTER SEVEN

Quality Schoolwork

It is important that we do not lose sight of what the goal of a Quality School is: all students doing increasing amounts of Quality Schoolwork. To achieve this, the students must feel very good about what they do in your classroom. (Feeling good about the work you do is the fifth condition of quality.) This will be achieved when you and they, together, have put the first four conditions of quality to work as you teach and they learn. Specifically, these conditions are that they:

1. know you and appreciate that you have provided a caring place to work;

2. believe the work you assign is always useful;

3. are willing to put a great deal of effort into what they do; and

4. have learned to evaluate their work and, from this evaluation, to make the effort to improve it.

Even if you are able to incorporate these four working conditions into your teaching, you should not expect many students to do quality work right away. Very few have ever even thought about working at this level in an academic class, and most of them will be making the effort to do quality work for the first time in their lives. Your job is to persuade them to continue this effort until they experience the joy of doing quality work. This will take patience: It is very important that you not be seen as nagging or threatening. Even before they attempt to do any quality work, you should try to persuade them to think about quality and how good any quality they may now have in their life feels.

To do this, I suggest that you wait for a time in your teaching when something of quality that would interest them comes naturally into the conversation—for example, either you or they mention a movie that most of them have seen and that you know many of them liked. Use this as a lead-in to involve them in a discussion of quality. **Keep in mind that they know what quality is, but they do not associate it with school.** If you can get them to talk to you in class about it, they will begin to think that there is a connection between school (you are school to them) and quality. For students in a beginning Quality School, this is a very necessary new idea.

After this discussion, no matter what grade you teach, you might conduct a quality "show and tell" in which any student can bring anything that he or she thinks is quality to show, or demonstrate, to the class.

For example, a music tape, a picture of a pet, a piece of art or jewelry, any collection, an antique or picture of an antique, or a poem. Students would also be encouraged to nominate a friend or teacher and tell the class why this person is quality for them.

In some classes this idea might fall flat. I suggest you try it, evaluate it, and see what you can learn. If you find a better way to persuade them to think about quality, let me know so I can share it with the consortium members in a reference bulletin.

You might also take advantage of their constant interest in knowing more about you by showing them something you have done that you believe is quality and telling them how good it felt when you did it. Then, using the Socratic method, discuss this with them and try to get them to figure out what made what you did quality for you. Ask them, "Would this have been quality for you?" If they are interested, continue by pushing the discussion toward why it would be quality for some and not for others.

When you believe they have begun to grasp the idea of quality, ask them to try to do a small amount of Quality Schoolwork. Tell them what you want is not your evaluation of this work but theirs. Say, "I want you to show me the work and tell me why you believe it is quality." Explain that they should feel free to take their time: You are not in a hurry. Tell them that you, and any assistants you may have in your class, are prepared to help them.

My guess is that the first bit of quality academic

work that most students will try to achieve is to write something that is far better than they have ever written before. Writing is a good starting assignment. I believe that quality writing is one of the two academic skills (quality speaking is the other) that have the highest correlation with success in life. Because writing is so tangible, it is easier to begin with writing than speaking.

Good writing leads to success because it requires that students be able to read, comprehend, think, evaluate, and then clarify their thoughts. When they believe they are able to do this, they will experience a feeling of intellectual confidence and competence that few students now possess. I have spent the last six years talking to well over three hundred high school students in depth, and I base the previous opinion on what I have learned from this experience.

If your students are having their first Quality School experience in a high school or middle school, they will have been writing for years, and many will think that they know how to write fairly well. After they have discussed quality and have begun to realize how different it is from what is ordinary or good enough, it may still come as a surprise to them that they may have never written anything that they would be able to judge is quality. When they finally write something that, to them, is obviously superior to what they have done before, they will experience a mixture of surprise and amazement and will feel good in a way that they have never felt before in school. Following the fifth condition of quality, **they will want to feel it again. Your goal is**

this initial bit of quality work. Once achieved, it has the potential to get the quality process started.

For this to happen, it is necessary that you persuade them to evaluate their work. If this is their first experience in a Quality School, it is likely that this will be the first time they have ever been asked to do this in a conscious, purposeful way. They are used to doing enough to earn a grade that will satisfy you and their parents so that they don't have to think about it any more. Self-evaluation is the only way to overcome the "**Do it as fast as you can, get the grade you want, and go ahead**" that is the work ethic of the traditional student.

To teach them to evaluate their writing, I suggest you talk a little about how they might do it and then give them a short, interesting paragraph from a good writer; or you may want to write one yourself. Make sure that the paragraph has a few serious flaws. (Good writers are not perfect writers.) Read it with them and then conduct a short discussion and try to get them to identify the flaws. As they do, write their suggestions for improving it on the board. Initially, don't push for more, just identify some of the improvements they all agree on. If they disagree, as they may, try to explain that there is no one road to quality. While improvement is the key, it can follow different roads.

The next day, provide them with a new paragraph, and pair them into two-student groups. Ask each pair to work together to try to look for more flaws and then to cooperate and work out a way to improve what they have found. Have some or all of the pairs present what they found and what they did. What you are trying to achieve is the idea that we can evaluate and improve what others do in order to learn ourselves.

From this, you could ask each of them to write a short paragraph. If they get interested and want to write more, that would be fine. Be ready to suggest a topic. Don't take a chance that they will be able to find something of interest on their own. Tell them that if they don't like your suggestion, it is fine with you if they want to write about something else. This approach keeps them from floundering, but at the same time it respects their need for freedom, a good way to do things in a quality classroom.

This will be a hard assignment, and I suggest that you ask them not to work too long the first day. Try to stop them while they still want to work, and tell them that if they can't wait until the next day, they should continue at home. This will give them the idea that homework is self-assigned, never compulsory, and that it is an opportunity for them to use their own time to do quality work. Tell them that spelling and even grammar is not as important as trying to say something interesting.

If they want to work at home, tell them you have no objections if they wish to enlist the aid of a parent. But let them know that in class, they will be asked to tell you, or one of your assistants, why they think this is a good paragraph. Even if they got parental help, this would make clear that they need to understand why the help made the paragraph better. Collect the paragraphs and read them over, not to grade them, but to get an idea of the level of their writing.

The next day, hand their paragraphs back and ask them to get into pairs. Each student should read the other's paragraph and then tell the other what he or she believes would improve his or her paragraph and why. Ask the other if he or she agrees. You might then ask them to work together to find at least one more way to improve what each wrote and to rewrite the paragraph, incorporating the suggestions. Pick them up again and reread them to see if they are catching on. That might be enough for this paragraph, but if they want to keep working on it, let them go ahead.

Do not grade these paragraphs. Grades tend to turn the process off because the students work for your grade instead of for their own judgment of quality. Tell them that all you want is improvement and that it is important that they, not you, be the judge of how much they have improved the original paragraph.

I hesitate to suggest any more. What I am trying to explain is how important it is to figure out how to get the process started. Quality does not happen: It has to be carefully nurtured into existence by a lead-manager who understands that getting the uninitiated started is a long, slow process. You may have something better in mind than what I have suggested, but I think that what I have outlined will provide you with a framework that includes the following steps:

1. Discuss quality enough so that they have a good understanding of what it is.

2. Figure out an assignment (it is better to begin with a skill like writing a paragraph) they agree is useful enough so that it is worth the effort to do well.

3. Ask them to work hard on the assignment by themselves and to do what they believe is a quality job.

4. Do not grade any quality assignment: A good grade stops the process because the student says, that's good enough, and a poor grade stops the process by discouraging the student.

5. Ask them to improve it and, to help them to do this, ask them to explain to another student and/or to you or to a teaching assistant, why what they have done has improved it.

6. In the beginning settle for improvement: Don't push for quality. Once they see the value of improving what they do, quality will come.

To move this quality procedure from a skill like writing into a subject area such as science, you might use a unit like weather and focus on hurricanes. No matter how you taught the unit, you would be wise to follow the above steps, starting with step one, the discussion of quality. Then you would take the time to discuss the weather and try to persuade them knowledge of weather is useful. There are a variety of ways for you to do this, such as watching a video of the local weather people and then breaking into groups of four and asking each group to produce a weather report on video.

They would be encouraged to be creative and humorous but at the same time not only to present the weather but to explain it. They could do much of the planning in school, but the production could be at home. There are plenty of video cameras around to do this. It is even possible that a local weather person could be invited to class to act as a resource person. If this person liked some of the videos, some of the students might get an invitation to appear on a local channel to do the weather.

For your students, the whole point is to move them from the mindset that school is covering ground to the new mindset of Quality Schoolwork. As quality is mostly achieved through cooperation, you would continually encourage them to help each other and to ask for help from you or anyone else. Quality is rarely a do-it-yourself process; there is no shame in asking for help. The competition is with oneself as each student works to improve what he or she does. With some sarcasm, Deming says, "We have learned that competition solves problems, competition is best for us, best for everybody. We've been sold down the river by economists who thought that competition is the way of life, the way to go. It is not. Will we ever learn?"[6]

CHAPTER EIGHT

Teaching the Nonacademic Skills

Experience proves that anyone who attempts to make major changes in the traditional "learn what we say or we will punish you" system will quickly be accused of being soft on basic academics. I have emphasized academics in this book, not only because I believe in them but also because I want to make sure that this accusation will not hold water if it is leveled at a Quality School. Even though the traditional system has failed miserably in the area of academics for well over half the students who finish school and almost no students do quality academic work, this criticism can frighten administrators and school boards. I plead guilty to bending over backwards to defend against it.

By now, with so many schools attempting to become Quality Schools, people very friendly to Deming and me are asking, "What place do the arts and vocational education and intrascholastic athletics play in a Quality School?" I will not discuss competitive, intrascholastic athletics, as this is usually an area of quality or attempted quality in a traditional school. That coaches who lead-manage rather than boss-manage tend to win more games is worth thinking about, but whether a school fields a winning or losing team will not affect the future lives of more than a few students. In this chapter, I will address art, music, drama, and the vocational skills: These should be very much a part of a Quality School because they are very much a part of all our lives.

In traditional schools, students are exposed to these skills, and those who are interested can pursue them to a considerable extent. More than athletics, they are among the highest quality of all the work that is done by students in a good traditional school. I noted with great satisfaction that in the summer of 1992, the orchestra of a local high school, Santa Monica, was selected as the best high school orchestra in the world at a contest in Vienna, Austria. No one would deny that for these students this has been a quality educational experience that they will never forget.

What is so important about art, music, and drama is that there is no doubt in anyone's mind that to pursue them seriously is to pursue quality, but students are rarely if ever counseled to pursue them seriously in traditional schools. On the other hand, students by the millions are counseled, even forced, to take academic subjects like math and history. Beyond passing them, no one really expects more than a few students to pursue these subjects seriously or to the point of doing quality work, and few, if any do. In minds of most citizens, math and history, even poorly learned, are more important than the arts. This is unfortunate, because in the real world, there are huge numbers of jobs in the arts. Entertainment (all art) is our biggest export, yet we downgrade these subjects in school.

What will be different about a Quality School is not that academics are more or less important than the arts but that, whether the students are pursuing academics, the arts, or both, the emphasis is on quality. What students need to get from school is the confidence, based on personal experience, that no matter what they choose to do, they can do a quality job. This is what our traditional schools lack, and part of this lack is that students who might be easily introduced to quality through the arts are rarely given a chance.

I may be wrong, but I am willing to bet that many of the young people in the Santa Monica orchestra are doing better academically because they are members of that quality music group. Closing down music programs to save money, as may happen in many schools in California from 1993 onward because money is short, will reduce the number of students, already too low, who are doing well academically.

What the arts, especially music and drama, do is introduce people naturally to a cooperative system. To quote Deming, "A great system is a great orchestra. What makes it great? Good players? Of course. Best in the country? Not necessarily, just good players. And they are managed. Every player is there to support the other 139 players. No player is there as a prima donna.... The orchestra is great because of cooperation."[7] To achieve this in both academia and in the arts is the teachers' job as lead-managers. But to do that job in academics in a Quality School, the students have to learn to work together. For many students, the easiest way to teach them to do this is to use the arts.

Even art itself (drawing, painting, illustrating) can be taught cooperatively. I have been in countless classes where the teacher has involved the students in a mural where they all work together to get the result they want. Singing together, playing music together, putting on a play which may require costumes, sets, music, lighting, carpentry, acting, reading (to select a script), or even writing an original play, all coordinated by the director (who is a good manager), can involve every aspect of education. School plays are usually outstanding; quality is apparent in every part of the production. Drama, therefore, would be commonplace in a Quality School because, in using it, so much can be learned by so many about quality.

The difference between a traditional school and a Quality School where the arts are concerned is that much more effort would be made in a Quality School to get all the students involved in the arts. Music, art, drama and even the practical arts would not be neglected or downgraded. For the skills needed to teach the arts that the staff does not possess, the school would reach out to the community. (I will discuss this more in a later chapter on community involvement in a Quality School.) All teachers would be asked to contribute their artistic teaching skills to the school. It would be good if

84

the budget could afford specific teachers, such as a music teacher, but, if not, the talent on the staff would be tapped. Most staffs have more talent than is apparent. As it emerges, teachers, if they were willing, would be used in as many classes as could be worked into the schedule.

An attempt would be made to link the arts with academics not only in drama, where they obviously go together, but, for example, in math, which it could be shown to be useful in music and poetic meter. Painting could be taught with history, as the history of the world is dramatically reflected in much great art. In science and anthropology, the cave drawings of France could be introduced; the number of these links is far more numerous than I could possibly know. The more links, the more likely it is that students would begin to see that quality, which is both obvious and necessary in the arts, is also a necessary part of academics.

VOCATIONAL SKILLS

When I ask students about the value of the academic courses they have to take to get through a traditional school, almost all of them tell me these courses are of little use in the real world. Even the few who see them as useful will not say they are directly useful. No student yet has admitted to me that he can see how he will use high school history, algebra, literature, or science after he leaves school. They do say that these courses are tickets to college or to a diploma that will help them

get a job, both of which are very much a part of students' real worlds. There is nothing unusual about this:
It is the way the traditional system has worked for over
a hundred years, and it is accepted as a normal function
of traditional schools that can't be changed.

With its emphasis on usefulness and quality, a Quality School will be seen by many more students to be a
very good ticket to college or to a job. Unfortunately,
they may still see it more as a ticket to a better future
**than as something real that is good for them right
now.** I believe we need to do even more than teach useful academics if we are to persuade many more students
that, right now, school is very good for them. While
what I am going to suggest is dramatic, we need something dramatic to call students' attention to the fact that
we are doing something very different and much better
in a Quality School. In time, I would like to see it
become a part of every Quality High School and, maybe
in a smaller way, a part of every Quality Elementary and
Middle School. I will, however, limit what I will now
describe to the high school, because this is the natural
place to start.

Among my own children and their friends, all of
whom are between twenty-five and forty-five years of
age and most of whom are quite successful, few know
much about how to deal with the many practical, everyday problems of living in a dwelling that is a part of all
of our lives. If they are not lucky enough to have a parent to show them, they go through life not even understanding how things like plumbing work, much less

being able to deal with them. (My life has been easier because my father and his best friend taught me a great many useful things.) These are skills and information that I believe should be taught to everyone who wants to learn them.

I suggest that every year, or every other year, if one year is not enough time, each Quality High School should buy a run-down house, or maybe a small, decrepit apartment building. It would then be a school project to teach as many students as wanted to be involved (all would get a chance to do something) how to renovate it. Then, at the end of the year or two years it took to finish the job, they could sell it and use the profit to pay for materials like computers or lab equipment or anything else the students and faculty decide was needed.

The project would be financed by a local bank, which would not refuse, as there would be no risk: The value would probably be doubled by the work that was done. There would be insurance problems but nothing that could not be worked out if the community united behind this educational project.

A teacher-supervisor would be needed, but a retired contractor-craftsman who likes kids can usually be found in any community. Once the word got out, I think the school would be flooded with qualified applicants. Local trade unions would probably be willing to provide instruction and supervision. The word would get out because this is just the kind of thing that the local media eat up. Besides doing the work, students would study the project from beginning to end so that they would get in-depth experience in a variety of practical areas.

For example, as a summer school project, one group would locate the house and go to the bank to get the financing. In the fall, another large group would be responsible for design, drawing the plans, and getting the building permit. Other groups would buy the tools and supplies, learn how to do the necessary construction, design the interior and decorate, landscape, and then taking turns on weekends sit at the house until it sold. If students were at the high school for four years, they could rotate through many of the jobs and graduate knowing more about the real world than they would ever know if all they had were the academics of a traditional school.

The contractor-craftsman, teacher, and helpers would be paid from the profits when the house was sold. They would have to agree when they took the job to settle for no more than an agreed percentage of the profits; there would be no possibility of the school's losing money. This would also provide an incentive to do a good job. It is not necessary for me to attempt to go into more detail here. There is nothing that could not be worked out if and when a project like this were authorized.

There are many spinoffs of such a project, all positive. For example, student volunteers could work weekends (always under supervision), which would give them something worthwhile to do that they don't have now. Working together is the best way to get to know and to like each other, and this would be a marvelous way to integrate the races that does not exist now in most schools. Students would get introduced to bookkeeping and accounting as they follow the flow of money expended. All the students could use this project as a practical basis for learning economics, a subject that for many of us seems at best to be arcane.

A project like this would be exciting for the school and bring the student body together in the best possible way through interesting and valuable work. Most of all, it would answer the constant criticism that our schools do not prepare students for the real world. It is also something students would remember and use for the rest of their lives, far more than they will ever remember or use much that they learn now. It would show the community that the Quality School they are paying for can involve students in tangible quality work because quality, more than anything else, would be needed for the project to succeed.

There is precedent for this project. The students of Mt. Edgecombe High School in Sitka, Alaska, one of the first schools in the world to embrace the teachings of Deming, run a full-fledged salmon smoking business and successfully sell the smoked salmon to support the school. Salmon smoking may be suitable for Alaska, but I am hesitant to suggest that a high school go into any regular business with so many people out of work. But renovating one house every year or two could not possibly do anything but provide a variety of economic benefits to any community.

CHAPTER NINE

Concurrent Evaluation

As long as we follow tradition, we accept the fact that no matter how much students learn, they do not get credit unless they pass the follow-up test. Conversely, if students pass the test they get credit no matter how little they learn. All of us are familiar with students who raise their hands and ask, "Is this going to be on the test?" as if only the material on the test is important. For many students, passing the test has become much more important than what is learned.

We are also familiar with teachers who asked questions on tests that were a complete surprise. These questions often did not even relate to what we studied, but teachers have the power to do this. Students become discouraged because they have no way to defend themselves against this unfair practice. On the other hand, we have all had teachers who were so predictable that we could easily anticipate what was going to be on the test, so this was all we made an effort to learn. Finally, we all are well aware that many students cheat, especially on "objective" tests, so no one has any idea what they really know. We need a new system of evaluation, because the current system depends far too much on test scores. You know that very often your test scores did not accurately reflect what you knew.

From the standpoint of the Quality School, what is so bad about traditional evaluation goes further than these obvious flaws: It does not lead students to do Quality Schoolwork. Concurrent evaluation, the system I will offer in this chapter, has the potential to correct this serious deficiency, but to make this change will not be easy. It will take courage to abandon the most ancient of all our educational traditions—teach, test, and then rank students by the test scores.

If you have the courage, you will be rewarded by the fact that concurrent evaluation is less work. You will not have to make up tests or grade them, yet it will be a much more rigorous system of evaluation that what you use now. As students begin to do quality work, it will eliminate any reason to rank students, which, if you are a dedicated teacher, is at best a painful process. As Deming says, "No one, child or other, can enjoy learning if he must be constantly concerned about grading and gold stars for his performance, or about rating on the job. Our educational system would be improved immeasurably by abolishment of grading and forced ranking."[8]

What you will find the most difficult if you move to concurrent evaluation is to give up formal testing, especially the use of the objective tests that are the backbone of traditional education. If we are to have quality, this is necessary, because tests and testing procedures persuade very few students to work hard. Even good students tend to do only as much as they think is needed to get the grade they want on the test. The majority of students, however, are not good students. They do poorly on tests, become discouraged, and, by middle school, make little effort to do more than get by.

Frustrated by these low performing students, traditional teachers uniformly resort to coercion. They threaten with low grades and failure. As the record clearly shows, this doesn't work. Despite being threatened and punished, over half the students who attend public schools do very little: They don't believe that making much effort in school is worth it. To persuade students like these to do competent schoolwork and even to think about doing Quality Schoolwork is a huge step ahead of where we are now. Concurrent evaluation is what we need to help us take this step.

Most politicians, and top educators like state superintendents, mindful of a dissatisfied public, are convinced that we need more mass testing to pinpoint what is wrong and that then, armed with this information, we will be able to improve the way we teach. They are willing to spend millions of dollars to find out what we already know: Huge numbers of intellectually capable students haven't learned enough in school to read a paragraph and pick out the key idea, write a good letter, and/or solve a thoughtful math problem. Colleges and employers have been telling us this for years.

What we lack is not more information from tests or any other source. It is the will to abandon our traditional "teach, test, rank, and coerce the losers" system of education, which, at best, does not work for more than half the students. If quality schoolwork is what we want, it fails many more than half. Nevertheless, because so few students do quality work, we should not be fooled into believing that only these few students can do quality work. All students are capable of doing it. That so few do only means that the system we have used for ages to teach and evaluate has nothing to do with quality.

For example, when I was talking with high school students in Alma, Michigan, in 1991, I asked my usual question, "Do many students in your school make an effort to do quality work?" This question had been preceded by a discussion of quality, so the students had a good idea of what I was talking about. A high school senior impressed the large audience when he stated that he had been mostly an "A" student and that everyone— his teachers, parents, and college admissions officer— was well satisfied. He then went on, "But I have never, in any class at any time, done the very best I can do."

From the discussion, he had quickly figured out that, although he had worked hard enough to get good scores on "their" tests, it was not quality. If we are to persuade not only students like this young man but all students to do quality work, we must **involve them deeply in the process of evaluating their own work as they do it: This is concurrent evaluation.**

It is unlikely that this young man's teachers had ever

involved him in evaluating his own work **as he did the work.** He had gone to school for twelve years and never yet done the best he was capable of doing. If I had not brought up the subject of quality, it would never have occurred to him to make this honest self-evaluation and reveal it. He is only one of the vast majority of the good students in our traditional schools who, evaluated the usual way, after they do the work by a test (usually "objective"), are rarely persuaded to pursue the quality we need if we are to be an economically competitive society.

CONCURRENT EVALUATION

To explain concurrent evaluation, let me use math, a subject in which few students now excel. Taught as it usually is, most students don't work hard because no one has persuaded them that math is a useful skill. We are wrong if we think they can figure this out for themselves. They complain that the class work and homework are boring and the tests difficult, and we have ample evidence that many graduating seniors are not even competent in arithmetic, much less math.

While I could use any grade level, I think you will best understand what I am trying to explain if I use a class taking ninth grade math for the first time in a new Quality High School as the basis for my explanation. In this school, all ninth graders would be required to take math, but the course would not be designated as any branch of math, such as algebra; it would just be math. Assuming that the students came from traditional schools and that **you are satisfied** that a good middle school general math textbook and a good ninth grade algebra text are available, the teacher would begin by asking all the students to start at the beginning of the general math book and see how far along in the book they thought they were proficient. As soon as they came to a group of problems they could not solve, they would mark that place and stop. If they believed they could solve all the problems in the general math book, they could go on to the algebra book and see how far they could go in that book until they came to problems they could not solve.

The teacher would circulate and help them with this initial assignment. By the end of the first week, every student should be able to find the furthest place in one book or the other where he or she felt proficient. A few would stop at the beginning, with addition and subtraction; many would be in the midrange between simple arithmetic and algebra; a few would be part of the way into the algebra book. It would be assumed, in this progressive subject, that students would be proficient in all the math processes that came before the place where they stopped, but this could and should be easily checked. It would pay to take the time to find out the exact place in math where each student is proficient. This is not wasted time, even if it takes several weeks.

Once it was determined where they all were, the class would be separated into groups of about four to six students. I believe an effort should be made to have low, middle, and high students in each group, but some teachers might want to group them separately. Either would work, but since students would be asked to help each other, it makes more sense to group students who know more with those who know less.

The students would then be told that there will be few, if any, formal tests and no compulsory homework: Their progress will depend on what they do in class. Each student would work alone to try to move ahead in the book, but all students would be told, "If you get stuck, ask another student in the group, who is ahead of you, for help." They would be told that they can move at their own pace. If they want to go faster, they can also work at home, but that all that is required is to work hard during this math period, which would be timed to last between forty-five and fifty minutes. Experience with this procedure has shown that, treated this way, almost all students are willing to work hard enough to make good progress.

SHOW AND EXPLAIN (SE), ACHIEVING COMPETENCE

Students would be told that when they believed they had mastered a group of problems in the book, such as long division, decimals, or the order of operations by doing enough of the odd-numbered problems correctly (assuming the odd problems were answered in the back of the book), they should call over the teacher or a teaching assistant. (In the next chapter I will explain how the teaching assistants, vital to a Quality School, would be recruited.) **Show** that person how they can work an even-numbered problem in the same group of problems. Then, if they were able to solve the problem correctly as the teacher watched, the teacher would ask them to **explain** why they did what they just did.

Showing and explaining (SE) how to solve a problem correctly as soon as they were confident they could do this would be the **evaluation, and it would always be concurrent.** To move on in the book, it would be necessary to be able to do this with each type of problem as it was encountered—no skipping. Now, many students go into a test without knowing how to work some of the problems that have been "covered" in class. If these problems are not on the test, the student passes the unit and may never learn how to solve this type of problem. Students who pass a test that omits a problem they don't know how to solve think they are lucky, and many go into tests hoping to get lucky. Using concurrent evaluation, none of this could happen: Luck would play no part in determining what they knew.

Teachers would make it their business to circulate and keep track of students' progress. They would look for students who were having trouble with a certain type of problem and were not getting the help they needed from the other students at their table. They would ask these students to meet with them in a small group for special tutoring, and most students would appreciate this concern and pay attention. The rest of the class could attend to their business and not be involved in a lesson they did not need or were not ready for.

All of this could be supervised by the student teaching assistants: Teachers would be available to help these assistants as needed. This is one of the strengths of this method. When students help each other, whether they do it informally as members of a small working group or as teaching assistants, they learn far more than if they just do their own work and do not teach or help others.

Most teachers would supplement the problems in the book with their own material and teach students to solve these problems as if they were from the book. Students would never be asked to solve a problem for the teacher until they were ready. If teachers gave tests, as some teachers still might do, the students would not be graded on how many they got right but would be asked to keep working until they got all the problems right and could both show and explain to the teacher or an assistant how they did them.

Some students would elect to do homework on their own to move ahead faster, to learn material that was not in the book or, in most cases, to catch up. It might be embarrassing to be too far behind, and the teacher might even counsel these students to do a little at home. Since the teacher and students would always be on good terms, students would tend to listen to the counsel of their teacher. The teacher could give highly interested students special time to encourage them to move to areas of math, such as theory, where it is possible to do quality work. Teachers would not work harder than now, and the work they did would all be directly helpful to students. Students would not sit around waiting for others to catch on or begin to panic as they got still further and further behind. No one would be ahead or behind; all would be moving ahead at their own pace.

Using concurrent evaluation, students gain confidence and grow to like math because, as far as they go, they really know what's going on. I believe that many more than now would move into higher math, such as calculus, if math, taught this way, were required through the eleventh grade, as it might be in a Quality School. Regardless of how far they got, all students would be able to show and explain what they have learned: There would be no doubt in anyone's mind how much they know.

GRADING

Although concurrent evaluation would work well without grades, grades may be too deep-seated a tradition to be eliminated. For example, if **all** a student were competent in by the end of eleventh grade math (when this type of student would likely elect to stop taking math) was math up to but not including algebra, he or she should get a "B" grade and credit for general math. I believe almost all students would know this much math before the end of the eleventh grade. Students who did not know this much math (really arithmetic) should show no math credit on their transcript and probably not graduate high school with a regular diploma until they did.

If high school students knew algebra or beyond well

100

enough to **show and explain** all aspects of the higher math process, they should get an "A" for as far as they went. Many would go far beyond beginning algebra. There would be no grades below an "A" for these competent students: Their transcript would record how far they went as "A" math students. For example, even if all they were competent in was algebra by the time they graduated, they would still get an "A" in algebra **because they would know it.**

If a teacher determined that a student, for some reason, could not do the math (or any subject in a Quality School), that student would be considered a special case and be graded as the teacher or the professional staff thought best. In some cases it might be wise to graduate such a student with some special indication on his or her diploma that there were some deficiencies but that it was still deemed that graduation was the right thing to do. It is impossible for me to do more than indicate what might be done with these few students; it will be up to each school to figure this out.

The reason that I chose to use math to begin to illustrate concurrent evaluation is that it is a logical, progressive subject. At the K-12 level, there is usually only one way to solve a math problem and, most of the time, only one right answer. When a student **showed** his teacher (or teaching assistant) how he did the problem and then **explained** accurately what he did, **in math this would show both competence and quality.** There would be no reason for most students to do more in math than be competent, so in this subject, **and in this subject alone,**

competence and quality would be the same thing, and they should earn an "A" grade.

Other academic subjects, such as English, history, science, geography, social studies, and health (as well as math, for the few top students who want to go into theory) provide students with much more of an opportunity to do quality work than is provided by regular math. For example, there is usually a clear difference between a competent essay and a quality essay, between a competent science project and a quality science project. In a traditional school, the work done by students in advanced placement (AP) classes is an example of work that is usually clearly superior to the work done in regular classes. In these subjects, if all a student was willing or able to do was to **show and explain,** the student would be awarded a "B" grade for competence.

FROM COMPETENCE TO QUALITY: SIR

S stands for Self-evaluation;

I for Improve what has been done;

R for Repeat the process until quality has been achieved.

As **self-evaluation** is a requisite for moving to quality, all students would be taught to **evaluate** their own work and, based on that evaluation, to **improve** it and to **repeat** this process until they began to do some of what they and their teacher would call quality work. It would not be expected that it would all be quality, but, considering how little quality work is done now, even some would be a good start.

For example, if they were satisfied with mastering the basics in a science course, such as chemistry, and could prove it by both showing and explaining, they would earn a "B," a competent grade. As explained, however, **these less structured courses would provide students with the opportunity to go beyond competence to quality.** They would achieve quality when they could show and explain that they had done a lot of **self-evaluation** and had **significantly improved** what they had initially done. If, through this improvement, what they now were able to accomplish was clearly superior to what was competent, they would have satisfied the main criteria for quality and would earn an "A" grade.

In keeping with modern evaluation practices, students would be encouraged to keep a portfolio of their work, but in a Quality School, **all they would be asked to keep in their portfolio would be examples of quality work:** work they had achieved through a lot of self-evaluation and repeated improvement. Even competent or good work would not be saved, so the portfolio would usually be small, as it would represent only quality work. On every piece of this work, students would be asked to write a short final evaluation stating why it was in their portfolio. The material would serve as a constant reminder to the student that he or she is capable of performing at this level.

To summarize, using concurrent evaluation, the emphasis in all courses would be to learn **all** the required subject matter and then to attempt to move to quality by going beyond what was required. This is in sharp contrast to the goal of a traditional school, which is to get a good grade on the test whether the work is quality or not. As stated, even a small amount of quality work should earn an "A," but it would be up to the teacher, with the help of the students, to decide if what was done was worth an "A." If students wanted an "A" but the teacher did not think that an "A" was warranted, the teacher would work with the student to help him or her figure out what more was needed to earn an "A."

For taking a lot of **initiative** that resulted in work of unusually high quality, students could be awarded an "A+" grade. Another way to get this top grade would be to act as a teaching assistant. Such grades or special awards would provide valuable recognition for college or for a job.

Art and practical art courses would fit perfectly into concurrent evaluation because in these courses concurrent evaluation is already frequently used. Also, in these elective courses (and athletics), many students do quality work now. For example, in most high school music courses, students show their teachers what they can do and, if it is unusual, explain why they played or sang the way they did. Improving the process through days and days of rehearsal with each student responsible for evaluating his or her own performance is a standard and highly effective procedure.

When we go from school into the real world of work, a lead-manager expects that the workers will show, explain, evaluate, and constantly improve what they do. Deming makes this point over and over in a variety of ways. Therefore, what I am suggesting in this chapter is what works so well in life. We should do the same in school.

Let me finish this chapter with a short summary of concurrent evaluation that you can use for quick reference.

SESIR, *THE ACRONYM FOR THE NEW SYSTEM OF CONCURRENT EVALUATION*

To achieve quality work, with or without the help of a teacher, I believe we need to embrace the five following processes:

S **Show** someone who is interested, such as a teacher, what we are doing. Do it carefully and completely so that this person can easily see that this is what we did.

E If it is not obvious or if there are questions, **explain** to that person how we achieved what we are showing him or her.

S After we do this, we evaluate (**self-evaluate**) what we did to see if it could be improved.

I   Most of the time it is obvious that we could
improve what we are doing, so we continue
working to try to improve it.

R   We **repeat** the evaluation and improvement
process, with or without help, until we believe
that further attempts at improvement are not
worth the effort. At this time, we believe we
have done what deserves to be called quality.

From kindergarten through the twelfth grade these
same five processes, **SESIR,** would be the way to teach
and evaluate in a Quality School. Students would learn
much more than now and begin to do quality work. In
an atmosphere free from both the fear and the restric-
tions of strictly graded, formal tests, students would be
better able to appreciate that education can increase the
quality of their lives, and teachers would find their job
much more enjoyable than they do now. Adopting
SESIR would also save the millions of dollars that we
continue to spend on mass testing in a vain effort to
coerce both students and teachers into doing "better."

CHAPTER TEN

Expanding the Classroom Staff

In an **ideal** world, if you wanted to become **competent** in something you did not know, you would seek an expert teacher who could give you a great deal of personal attention. You would not mind if there were a few other students, but you would not select a teacher who had twenty-five to forty students in his or her classes. An expert teacher would show and explain the subject, answer your questions as they arose, point out where you needed specific help, give it to you and, throughout, treat you with warmth and courtesy.

You would expect the teacher to ask you to show and explain what you had learned so that both of you would have a good idea of your progress. From both your own and your teacher's evaluation of your competence, you would be able to decide that you had learned what you set out to learn. You would also expect to find out a little about the teacher personally and, one hopes, you would like what you found out. Taught this way, you would not only become **competent** in a reasonable amount of time, but, **because it would feel so good to be taught this way,** you would also begin to think in terms of quality. **We do not live in an ideal world** and are far from achieving **competence,** much less quality, with most students. But it is fair to say that if we achieved at least competence, almost everyone would be satisfied. **In K-12 education, few educators at any level think beyond competence.**

Since quality learning goes well beyond competence, both teachers and students find it difficult even to conceptualize a Quality School.[9] Even though they know that almost all students have no desire to go further than competence, the staff of a Quality School will not settle for this minimal goal. From the start, they try to teach all the students to do increasing amounts of Quality Schoolwork so that they can experience the **joy** of learning: **the main motivator for hard work and the only motivator for quality.** If our students are to compete in today's highly competitive world of quality products and services, we have no choice but to push our goal forward from competence to quality. **The ideal world of yesterday has become the real world today.**

We cannot achieve quality unless we move much closer to the ratio I have just described as ideal—one teacher to a small group of students. The traditional class of twenty-five to forty students will not work. It is too impersonal and too large to implement **concurrent evaluation.** Much more personal attention than most students get is needed if we are to persuade them to self-evaluate, improve, and repeat the process (**SIR**) until what they have done in class is quality. Unless skilled assistants are available to help the teacher provide this attention, most students will not move to quality. If there are not enough teaching assistants, the students will have to wait too long for what they need. Waiting, many will grow bored and lose interest, and their movement toward quality will grind to a halt.

Since schools do not have the money for more paid teachers or teaching assistants, the staff of the Quality School will have to work out a plan to provide a great many additional personnel at no cost to the school system. How much help will be up to each of you as professional teachers to determine, but my estimate is that in a class of thirty students, at least three full-time assistants per class would be minimum. In some classes, such as writing, six might not be excessive.

This does not mean all assistants must be in place from the beginning. I would suggest first one; as you get used to this new way of teaching and your class to this new way of learning, slowly add others. It would be easy to determine how many were needed. As I have stated, I recognize that there is a lot for you to accept and assimilate in a Quality School, so I suggest that this new procedure be initiated slowly and carefully. There is no imposed timetable for any of the Quality School innovations.

All new procedures will have to be worked out together in the many staff meetings that you will need to get the Quality School process started and keep it going. You are no longer working alone in your class, as too often happens in a traditional school. What you do has an effect on everyone else—other teachers, students, and even parents. The more quality you achieve in your class, the easier it will be for other teachers to achieve it in their classes. Cumbersome as it may be, a Quality School depends on a democratic faculty working hard together and accepting each other. Within the faculty, there would likely be a series of committees. One such committee should be entrusted with working out ways to recruit the volunteer classroom teaching assistants needed.

While at first glance it would seem difficult to recruit a large number of volunteers, in practice this need not be so. There is a huge pool of easily trained, willing volunteers available in your school, neighboring schools, and the community, waiting to be tapped. Many of these people will already have the skill to do what is needed, but it is obvious that some sort of **training program** would have to be set up to make sure they were competent to do the job. They don't have to be skilled lecturers or make up lesson plans. They just have to have the skill to listen to students as they show and explain what they have learned and to help them to learn more individually or in small groups.

The competence needed by an assistant would vary from subject to subject. For example, it should be easier to find people able to assist in math than in English, as quality math requires only competence, quality English much more. Assistants who could work with students in writing courses would be the hardest to find, but if one reads the letters to the editor in newspapers, it is apparent they are there in large number waiting to be asked. Because their help would be so appreciated, the initial volunteers would spread the word. I am sure that a good number would be willing to drive into difficult neighborhoods. Ultimately, each teacher would be responsible to check the competence of assistants. In the beginning, this would take some time. Once done, however, the rewards in help to the teachers would far outweigh the effort to get the process started.

As indicated above, there are four main recruitment sources:

1. students in your own class or classes;

2. students in your school or in another school close by;

3. college students who are interested in a career in teaching or just interested in helping;

4. adults in the community who would like to help and who have the skills and time to help.

From these four groups, teachers, usually with the aid of parent volunteers to help access the adult group, should be able to enlist all the classroom help they need. Let me go through the four sources of help and make some suggestions as to how to go about recruiting what you need.

STUDENT HELPERS FROM THE TEACHER'S OWN CLASS OR CLASSES

This is the most available source of help. In any class of about thirty students, except maybe English, there are some who are quite gifted in the subject, especially in math and science. The number may be as high as ten or as low as two, but it is likely that about four or five students will be almost immediately recognized as highly knowledgeable at this level or beyond. As soon as you identify them, you should ask them if they want to help you by acting as teaching assistants. Arrange to meet with them individually if you want to start with one at a time or in a small group if you want to start with several.

Tell them that their job will be to check out any student who raises his hand signifying that he is ready to **show and explain** that, for example, in ninth grade math, he had learned to solve a problem at his level. If the student could do the problem, the teaching assistant would tell him to go ahead to the next group of problems. If he could not, the assistant would give the student instruction, ask him to practice more, and tell him to try again as soon as he felt he was ready. In the beginning, say for the first month, if the teaching assistant was satisfied that the student was competent, she would still call over the teacher to check her assessment of the student's competence. As soon as it became apparent that she was able to do the job, she would not call the teacher over for help unless she was unsure of herself.

The incentive for the student assistants is that they would be guaranteed an "A" grade and told that they would be eligible for an "A+" grade if they continued to do this satisfactorily for the whole year—assuming that they themselves had completed at least ninth grade algebra at a level of competence. Before a student could be accepted as an assistant to the teacher, he or she would have to get parental permission. All parents would be given a small booklet (written by the staff) explaining the teaching assistants' responsibilities. At the end of the year, the assistants would be given a special award, and, when they graduated, the extent of their help would be noted on their transcript and diploma.

Students could also be recruited from your other classes to act as assistants in any class. They could come from the same level or from higher levels. Their job would be to assist in one class only, giving up only a period a day or, if a lot of students were available, possibly a period or two a week. They would have no personal work responsibilities in this "extra" class and could devote more time to teaching than they would have if they were enrolled in the class.

Since students in a Quality School do not compete with each other, there would be no reason for petty jealousies to arise; in fact, it would be the opposite. Students would appreciate the help that was always available. Any student who worked hard and wanted to participate in the program could apply, and an effort should be made to give every competent applicant a chance. If the student was not skilled enough to assist at his own level—for example, a ninth grader assisting in ninth grade math—he might be able to assist in ninth grade math when he was a competent tenth or eleventh grade math student. To assist, however, in any subject except math, the assistant would have to show that she had done some quality work in the subject she was assisting in at that level or above. This would be a further incentive for students to make the effort to do quality work.

STUDENTS FROM OTHER CLASSES OR SCHOOLS

Since this teaching assistant program in a Quality School would be well known, teachers could nominate students to act as teaching assistants in classes other than those taught by the nominating teacher. Perhaps they would join a pool of assistants that would be maintained in the school from which all teachers could draw as needed. Teachers from neighboring schools who knew about the program could also nominate interested students who would go to the Quality School to assist whether or not their school was a Quality School. They, too, might become a part of the assistant pool, and training could be set up for the members of this pool in all the subjects where assistants were needed. Recruiting students from other schools to act as teaching assistants in a Quality School would also be good public relations and help the ideas of the Quality School to spread.

COLLEGE STUDENTS

The Quality School staff should work with colleges and college departments of education to recruit volunteer assistants. It is possible that colleges would even make this an elective course and give credit to students who volunteered. Volunteers need not be restricted to students who are interested in teaching as a career. Other students might be interested, especially in math and science, and they would be told that there is no better way to hone their skills than to do this kind of work. Once the word got out that this kind of volunteer work was available, I am sure that good schools like the Quality Schools, where there were no discipline problems, would be attractive enough so that there would be no shortage of volunteers.

ADULT VOLUNTEERS

In some respects this would be the most important group, and retired people would be the ones most interested. Retirees are not used enough anywhere, and, where they are, the work is often at a level far below their intellectual skills. Assisting teachers with teaching in the classroom, not with clean-up or record keeping, would not be beneath anyone and would be very attractive. Many older people, even some retired teachers, enjoy working with and getting to know young people. There is no better way to get to know anyone than to listen to what they have accomplished, as would be the case with concurrent evaluation. All people, young and old, hunger for closeness to others. The "cannot help but do well" atmosphere of a Quality School, where teachers and students feel good about themselves and where all who teach reveal themselves, is an ideal place for this closeness to develop.

The good part of using adult volunteers to help tutor and to work in the concurrent evaluation process is that once they signed on, they could be counted on over a period of time. The students would get used to them and would talk about how helpful they found them, which would give them the credibility that would make them increasingly effective. If you provide a good place for a person to volunteer, you are not exploiting them, even if they occasionally complain a little. In a Quality School, they would be getting as much as or more than they are giving.

As stated previously, it is important that in a Quality School no student ever sit in class and wonder what is going on or believe that "I can't improve" or that "I am a failure," all of which are common to students in a traditional school. The volunteer assistants would always be on hand to help any student who was stuck and, in doing so, would prevent this from happening. This quick help would also prevent the majority of discipline problems that too many teachers struggle with now. Students would be told that when they ask for help, they will get it quickly on a one-to-one basis in almost every class in a Quality School.

If possible, the Quality School should be open at night for classes to be taught by volunteers from the community who have skills and want to teach one or two nights a week. It would be especially powerful to offer courses that parents would want to take along with their children. When family members learn something together that they are both interested in, they develop a closeness that is special and important. For example, parents and students could take a computer course together; no one would doubt the value of such an experience. This course could even be taught by a student, as students who are computer whizzes are a part of every student body in most middle and high schools.

While there is no compulsory homework in a Quality School, night school could be a place where students could catch up by coming to remedial classes in the basic skills. Students could also get ahead or enrich themselves through small, noncredit advanced classes that would not be offered in the regular school because of budget constraints. A foreign language like Chinese, photography, video production, or computer graphics all taught by skilled volunteers are examples of what I mean. The only expense would be to pay for the utilities; all else, including fund raising, would be provided by volunteers. This could be a good use for some of the money that would be raised through selling the renovated house mentioned in an earlier chapter.

Evening athletic programs for parents and students would also be a part of the night school program, depending on the school's athletic facilities. Programs like these are available in many schools now, so this would be no departure from what is already well established.

COMMUNITY SERVICE

More than ever, programs for students to help in the community are now on the increase and should be a part of every Quality School. The school should make it known that it would be interested in working on any community problem and that any individual or organization could approach the school and ask for help. In a Quality School, a social studies class could study these community requests and make the decision as to whether the school should get involved. If students are to work, they should decide; no one should volunteer their services for them.

The only proviso would be that any service the students rendered to the community would have to have an educational component. Students would not be asked to volunteer for clean-up or any service activities unless that work and its benefit to the community were being studied and something useful could be learned from it.

STUDENT RESPONSIBILITY FOR THE PHYSICAL PLANT

Once the students become aware of how need-satisfying it is to attend a Quality School, they will put a picture of the school in their Quality Worlds. Once they do, they will be willing to take responsibility for maintaining and improving the physical plant. If we are to teach students responsibility, there is no better way to do this than to **make taking care of the school a subject to be studied and implemented.** Students should be involved in learning about how the school is financed and then be responsible for learning what their work is worth. They should not be told what to do but involved in helping plan what needs to be done. When they do it, they should figure out how much money was saved by their labor. If students refuse to work, they should be counseled, or, with their permission, this refusal should be discussed in a class meeting. No attempt should be made to force a student to work, as this would defeat the basic purpose of the school.

They should be encouraged to make the school sparkle with fresh paint inside and out. People driving by the school should be impressed by how well kept it is. The landscaping should be beautiful, there should be no litter, and part of the grounds could be made into a pretty little playground for preschoolers. Students could be involved in helping with the preschoolers and would use the playground to learn about child care. If this were valued by the community, it might be possible to earn some money for such school activities. The students would be challenged to do as much as possible with the plant and to figure out things to do that are not usually done with a school but could be of service to the community.

Different classes could be responsible for taking care of different areas, and this could rotate so students learned all aspects of custodial care. The custodial staff could serve as the teachers and managers on this project. Signs could be posted in the areas designating which class was responsible for the care of the area. Throughout the year there could be open house, where each class is responsible for explaining to visitors what they have done and what they learned from doing it.

The whole idea is to help students develop a sense of pride in what they have done to make their schools the best kept public buildings in the community. This pride is important. A quality society is clean and attractive. School should be a place where students learn to feel pride. Communities that see well-kept schools filled with disciplined students who are doing quality work will support these schools financially. They don't see this enough now, which is one reason why there is so little support for education. We must keep in mind that many people do not have children in school, and it is their support we especially need. When we do as suggested here, we will get it.

CHAPTER ELEVEN

Teaching Control Theory to Students

In a traditional school, when a child is in any kind of trouble the first suggestion is that he needs counseling. But if we depend on counseling, we find that there are too many students who need it and not nearly enough counselors available. If, however, the students know control theory, when they get into trouble they can figure out what is wrong and, with much less counseling, use what they have learned to solve the problem, whether it is a home or school difficulty. This is the big advantage of teaching control theory: It is usable knowledge, and it gives them a sense of control over their lives that they can't seem to get without it.

In a Quality School, therefore, I believe that teachers have the responsibility to teach control theory to students. Considerable information about this theory is *The Quality School.* For more, you might want to read the basic book on this subject, ***Control Theory.*** Although it is not mandatory, it is strongly suggested that all the staff of a Quality School follow the recommendations that are available from our office; they are also written into the revised 1992 edition of *The Quality School* (see Author's Note at the front of this book). This would mean that everyone who signed the contract would eventually have both weeks of the intensive training, much of it covering the control theory that is fundamental to all you would be doing in these schools. However, whether you have had this training or not, this chapter should give you many suggestions that will help you teach control theory to your students no matter what grade you teach. In writing this chapter, I am assuming that you have carefully read chapters four, five, and six of *The Quality School.*

Control theory is a new explanation of how we choose to live our lives: It is actually a new psychology. Once learned, we can use it profitably all our lives. Through it we should be able to get a much clearer understanding of how to manage, teach, and counsel more effectively than we do now. It also explains why what Deming suggests is so effective in managing students to do quality work. This is why my ideas and Deming's are so closely associated.

Many teachers, having learned this theory in order to teach it, report that they are now more successful in other areas of their lives besides their work. While this should be a powerful incentive to learn it, the main reason I want you to teach it to your students is that much of their ineffective and, at times, self-destructive behavior stems from not knowing how they function as human beings. If they knew, they would make an effort to work harder in school and generally be much more effective and happier as they lived their lives. As teachers like yourself have attempted to do this, they have asked many questions of me and my associates who have consulted in their schools. To answer these questions much excellent material has been written.[10]

Starting as early as kindergarten, each elementary school teacher should begin to explain the five basic needs and the concept of the Quality World. By the first grade, students are ready to learn what behavior is, that we choose it, and that all of our behavior is our best attempt at the time to control (not dominate) the world around us so that we can best satisfy the pictures in our Quality Worlds. The emphasis should be on the fact that we **choose** all we do and that we are all responsible for the choices we make. They should also be taught that it is their job to figure out the best choices.

For them to catch on to the ideas, it is good to use situations from your own life, such as how you use control theory to become a better parent. Tell them, for example, that last night you were angry and yelled at your daughter (or son) because she did not clean up her room, something they can all relate to easily. Talk about how you like all the rooms in your house neat and clean, and say that when you see a dirty room your need to survive (dirt is harmful) and your need for power (you are proud of the way you keep your house) are frustrated. This may also be a good time to teach them the important idea of frustration and what you mean when you use the word "frustrated."

Tell them that based on these two needs, you have a picture in your Quality World of your house neat and clean. But because you love your daughter, you are also frustrated when you yell at her, and you don't like yelling at anyone. Ask them if they can help you to figure out a better behavior than that. They might also suggest that maybe you would be wise to change your picture of your daughter keeping her room super clean, that she isn't going to do it and that you are just going to be upset a lot. If what they suggest makes sense, which is likely, try it. If it works, thank them for helping you to choose better behavior.

Working with students from second grade up, use examples from their classroom behavior, books, movies, television, and, if they are in elementary school, video cartoons to teach this theory. Ask them to bring cartoons from home. If they bring "The Three Little Pigs," show it and go through the needs of the pigs and the wolf and have them suggest the pictures to satisfy these needs that these characters store in their Quality Worlds. Then talk about their choice of behavior, which made the best choices, and why. Keep teaching this basic control theory. As they understand it, and get older and more sophisticated, teach them the concept of total behavior. Explain that they actually choose behavior like anger and depression, and point it out when they do. Also remind them that they have control over the pictures they put into their Quality Worlds and that sometimes it is wise to change one of these pictures, as you may have done with your daughter and her untidy room.

To help them realize how much it applies to them, use a situation from your class. For example, if four or five students create a ruckus on the playground, call the whole class together (in a circle) for a class meeting. Be sure to get the permission of the students who were involved in the ruckus and include them in the discussion. If you are going to talk about something that could upset their parents, you might want to clear it with them before you hold the discussion. Ask:

1. What is the behavior that each of these students chose?

2. What need or needs were they trying to satisfy with this behavior?

3. What was the picture in their Quality Worlds that they were trying to satisfy when they chose to start the ruckus? What need did that picture come from?

4. What better behaviors might they have chosen that would have avoided the ruckus?

5. What suggestions make sense to the students who were involved? Are they are willing to try them next time?

You can use these same questions when you counsel individual students, always teaching control theory as you work with them. Keep a little car on your desk called the "behavioral car," and when a student figures out a better behavior ask her what behavioral road she is steering her car down now. Keep emphasizing that they steer their lives; that it is their choice to do what they do; and that, if they make a poor choice, they can always make a better one. Later in this chapter, I will explain how you might do this in much more detail.

For many students, their first exposure to a Quality School will be in a middle school or high school, so this instruction in control theory would be delayed until that time. As they change classes in a secondary school, all teachers need not be responsible for teaching this. Perhaps health or science teachers, who volunteer, should be designated as the primary control theory teachers. All teachers, however, should attempt to bring control theory into their classroom discussions. They could speculate on what needs led to the pictures that both fictional and real people chose to put into their Quality Worlds that were the motivation for the behaviors they chose.

If your school has signed the contract to become a Quality School, obtain copies of the control theory material listed at the end of the book and check it out. Several years ago I wrote what is called the "Choice Program," an excellent program to teach students from fifth through ninth grades what control theory is. This program is based on students learning control theory and how it can help them to make better choices, including the choice not to use drugs. Information on the program is also listed at the end of this book. However you decide to teach it, keep in mind that there is no hurry;

this is and should be a long process. As long as you teach in a Quality School, never let an opportunity to teach this material slip by. This is true lifetime learning. None of us will ever get to the point where we have learned all there is to know about how we function.

As much as I recommend the special training and the use of the available materials, I also recognize that many teachers will find control theory easy to learn. There is no doubt in my mind that some of you will gain a great deal of expertise with it from the books and personal experience and through talking to friends on the staff who are also interested. Once you feel comfortable with it, you can use small, cooperative groups and encourage students to write and act out skits and do other things. What you will find that will encourage you is that students catch on to control theory quickly and enjoy learning it. As they do, they begin to see how it can be applied in their lives, and, for them, this is always exciting.

Finally, I would like to spend the rest of the chapter suggesting how control theory could be taught in a way that few teachers teach it now: using the classroom meeting as the format for teaching it. This would be open to teachers of all grades.

TEACHING CONTROL THEORY THROUGH CLASS MEETINGS

Assuming you are comfortable with the concepts of control theory, I suggest that you use every opportunity to teach it a little at a time through class meetings. For example, the most basic of the control theory ideas that will help students once they learn it is that all of our behavior comes from within ourselves and we choose what we do. For students, as for most people, this flies in the face of common sense: They do not believe that they choose much of their behavior, especially behavior that gets them into trouble. They believe that they can't help what they do; it is an automatic reaction or a response to what goes on around them. If, by the fourth grade, students could really understand that they choose what they do, they would be much better prepared to live their lives than they are now.

Let's take a common situation that will arise in almost all classes at all levels, and I will try to explain how you might use that example to begin to teach some basic control theory. Suppose there is a fight; one student hits the other, and the other hits back. Both are upset and blaming the other. The class sees the fight, everyone is aware of what happened, and most students have made up their mind that one of the students had to fight because he was provoked by the other; he had no other choice. That student claims I would never have hit him if he hadn't hit me, called me a name, insulted my family, took my property, cheated me, put me down, or accused me of something I did not do.

Although they do not realize it, the students are saying that they, like all the people they know, believe in stimulus-response psychology: Our behavior is a necessary and automatic response to what has happened to us, and we cannot be responsible for what others do. Your job in a Quality School is to teach them that their behavior is not caused by what happened to them. It is caused by what goes on **inside** their heads, and whatever they do, **they are choosing to do it.** They could have chosen something different if they wanted to.

Any student who learns this well enough to use it in his life has learned a valuable lesson, which, with the present wide access that very young people have to guns, could save his life. When the fight is over and all parties are calmed down because you have told them that you do not want to punish them or look for whose fault it is, try to teach the whole class how to avoid fights and how to get along better with each other.

THE FIRST MEETING

Get the class together in a circle and tell them that you want to help them learn something about that fight that they can use for the rest of their lives. Tell them you won't do this all in one day but that, over the next few weeks, you will occasionally take some time from class to begin to teach them control theory, which is a new theory that explains what they do and how they do it. They will like the idea of learning something new and probably pay attention, as most students welcome any change from routine. Tell them that, although you will be talking about the fight, this is only to teach them. You are not interested in going back and rehashing the occurrence in any detail.

Prepare for the first discussion by bringing a telephone (it could be a toy phone) to class. Make a ringing sound and then ask them, "What do you do when the phone rings in your house?" Go around the class and get an answer from almost every student. They will almost all answer, "Pick it up and say hello." If some answer something like "I keep sleeping," note this but don't comment.

Then go on and ask, "Do you always pick up the phone when it rings?" Some will say no but most will still say yes. Then ask, "If you are sure it is a person you don't want to talk to—suppose you owe that person money and you don't have it—would you still answer?" Now most will change their minds. Then ask what would you do if you didn't answer. You will get a variety of answers, such as "Let it ring" or "Ask someone else to answer, and say I'm not home." Listen to all the answers but don't comment except to say that there seem to be a lot of things you can do when the phone rings besides answer it.

Take a few more minutes to ask them some more questions about the same thing—for example, "Do you always cross in the crosswalk?" "Do you always brush your teeth?" "Do you always study for a test?" Then ask, "Is there anything you can think of that you always do no matter what?" Push this question and see if you can find something they always do. If you keep questioning, it is likely that they won't admit to **always** doing anything. Then make a small joke by asking, "Do you always breathe?" They will laugh but will say that this they always do. What you have done so far should take about twenty minutes.

If the class is very interested and wants to talk, give them a little more time but not too much time, no more than thirty minutes. Try to get students involved who haven't said much by saying things like, "C'mon, John, I know you have something to say." Or, "Sue, I saw you whispering to Janet, you're a good thinker, what was on your mind?" Push a little but not too hard, especially if the student is uncomfortable. End the meeting and say that in a few days we are going to talk about this again. Ask them to think about why they do anything and everything that they do. Do they do anything else as consistently as breathe? During the time between meetings, try to keep their interest by reminding them to keep trying to figure out if there is anything they do that they don't choose to do.

THE SECOND CLASS MEETING

Tell them that you want to talk more about choosing what they do and ask, "Except for breathing, is there anything you ever do that you don't choose to do?" They will struggle with this, but, if you act as the devil's advocate, in the end they will have to admit that all, except breathing, is chosen. Agree, tell them that you also believe that everything we do we choose, but then go on to ask, "Can anyone make you do anything that you do not want to do?"

Now they will say that many people can make them

do things they don't want to do—their mothers, fathers, grandmothers, big brothers, tough kids in the neighborhood, or anyone with a gun, to name a few. First focus on their contention that their mother can make them do things they don't want to do. Ask, "Haven't you disobeyed your mother lots of times?" You may get into an argument with them as they tell you, "Yes we have, but not when she finds out, then we have to do what she says." Keep questioning until they say that mostly they obey not because they have to or that she will punish them, but because they love her and they want her to love them.

Ask, "Do you obey people you don't love?" They will answer that they do if they are afraid of them and bring up the gun example again. Ask, "If someone with a gun asked you to give them all your money, might you sometimes take a chance and refuse? Even if you are afraid, couldn't you choose to risk your life to keep your money?" If they counter with, "That would be stupid," say, "Haven't you ever heard of people choosing to do stupid things like that and even getting killed?" They would have to say yes and you should agree with them by saying, "We all choose to do stupid things all the time."

Tell them you are trying to teach them that we choose to do everything we do. Sometimes we do things because we don't want to because we are afraid of losing someone's love, which would be worse. Other times, we do things we don't want to do because we are frightened and not doing them would be worse than doing them. Sometimes we do what we later find out is stupid, but it didn't seem so stupid at the time. But when we do something stupid, we don't like to admit that we chose to do it. Instead, we like to say, "I had to do it; I didn't have a choice; someone made me do it; I didn't realize what would happen; I took a chance." Ask, "If you do something smart, do you like to say that you chose to do it?" Discuss the difference between taking responsibility for doing stupid things and doing smart things.

Tell the class a few stupid things that you have chosen to do, such as eating so much that you became sick, or driving so fast that you got a ticket. Tell them what you told your friends in order to avoid admitting that you chose to do these stupid things. Ask them to reveal a few stupid things that they have done and what they said to avoid admitting that they chose to do them.

Then ask, "Is there any way to know if something you are about to choose is stupid?" Talk about this until they come up with the answer that, if we knew more about the whole situation, we might be able to make better choices. Agree with them and ask, "How do we learn more about the whole situation?" For example, say, "Some students choose to drop out of school, which they later admit was a stupid thing to do. At the time, they thought it was a good choice. Why do they make this choice?" To help them, ask the opposite question, "Why do some students never think of dropping out of school?" Continue with this line of questioning until they say that as long as we think we are learning things we can use in our lives, we stay. Agree with them and end the meeting.

THE THIRD MEETING

Review with them the new idea that they choose all they do. Sometimes they make good choices and sometimes bad choices, but they are all choices. Now ask, "Why do you get hungry?" They will answer that we need food to stay alive. Help them to figure out that hunger tells them that they need food. Ask what else do you need to survive, and they will come up with air, water, shelter, the basics. Then ask, "Have you ever gotten in a fight or a big argument because you were concerned that you would not survive if you did not argue or fight?" A few who live in very rough neighborhoods may say yes, but almost all will say no. Then ask, "If you don't argue or fight to survive, why do you argue and fight?"

Some will say that they don't like to be called bad names. Pursue this. "Why do you not like to be called a bad name? Or listen to someone call a person you love a bad name?" They will tell you that they don't like people running over them or putting them down. Ask why they choose to get angry when someone puts them down. They will argue that they don't choose to get angry, the person made them angry by calling them a bad name. Counter this with, if you don't choose it, how does it happen.

They will say it just happens, they can't help it. Counter this with, "Suppose someone very tough and much bigger puts you down? Do you get angry and start a fight knowing you will be beaten to pulp? Don't you choose to sulk or run away or get resentful but not very angry? You keep the anger down because if you got angry you might do something foolish like fight, and then you would get beaten or even killed. Sometimes, aren't you more scared than angry?" Continue this discussion until they understand that no one can make them angry or scared, that these too are choices, that everything is chosen.

Tell them that there are always good **reasons** they get frustrated (make sure they know what frustrated means) and then choose to do whatever they do, get scared or get angry. Tell them that these reasons are just like the reason they get hungry and ask, "Would you like to learn these reasons?" They will be interested and will either say yes or show through attention and expectation that they are interested.

Begin by asking, "If someone insults your best friend, why do you get angry? Or if a good friend rejects you, why do you get angry?" If you continue this discussion, they will say that they need their friends, they want to keep them and protect them. Tell them they are right, that we all need friends, and when something or someone threatens a friendship, we get frustrated and have to choose to do something. We choose to get angry or, if we are rejected, we choose to get depressed.

Ask, "Is it possible to not care, to pay no attention if a good friend rejects you?" They will say, "No, that would be impossible." Agree with them and tell them that the way we are built, the way our brain is constructed (point to your head when you say this, for emphasis), we need friends. Ask, "Do some people need more friends than other people?" Discuss this, and they will agree. Make the point that while we are all different to some extent in the number of friends we think we need, **we all need friends.**

Ask, "Is there anything else you need that is as strong as your need to stay alive and your need for friends?" and "Do you need people to listen to what you have to say?" Explain that in these discussions you are trying hard to listen to what they have to say. Ask, "How do you get people to listen to you, to respect you, to look up to you, to pay attention to you?" Discuss this until they get the idea that if they listen to others there is a good chance others will listen to them. This is a good time to digress a little and talk about the golden rule.

Explain that we all need a sense of power, which is satisfied by others respecting us and listening to us and not trying to insult us or push us around; that this is built into us just the same as the need for survival and love and friendship. To get them to think about the need for freedom ask, "Why do we get frustrated if people tell us we can't do something or go somewhere?" If you discuss this for a while they will answer that they need freedom and that, when their freedom is restricted, they get frustrated and may choose to get angry or fight or sulk or run away.

Finally, ask, "Do you like to laugh, play, joke, and have a good time?" Pursue this until they say that they like to have fun, that having fun is important to them. Ask them if they have ever risked their life just for fun and talk about parachute or bungee jumping and ask them to tell what they have done for fun that was risky. Talk for a while about how important fun is and what they like to do for fun. To make the point ask, "Do animals go after fun?" And when they say yes, ask for examples. Ask, "Do turtles or insects go after fun?" Talk about the difference between a dog and turtle and which goes after fun the most.

After this discussion, they will begin to get the idea that besides staying alive we need love, friendship, power, freedom, and fun. They will still think that staying alive is the most important need. Deal with this misconception by asking, "If staying alive is so important, how do people get up the courage to commit suicide?" Talk about suicide. Most of them will have known someone who killed himself or herself. Ask them, without identifying the person, what they thought was his or her reason for doing this. It will then be apparent that loss of love, mostly, but also loss of power or freedom causes some people to kill themselves.

Tell them that now we have talked about all the basic needs that determine the behavior we choose. Write these five needs on the board and leave them written on the board:

1. Survival (security)

2. Love and Friendship

3. Power (gaining and keeping respect)

4. Freedom

5. Fun

THE FOURTH MEETING

Put what they have learned through these discussions into practice by going back to the fight. Ask them to tell you the choices they often make now that get them into a typical argument or fight. Keep going after this until they go through many of the things they choose to do when they are frustrated. Then ask them about the needs that were frustrated, using the following questions:

1. Doesn't a fight (or argument) often break out when someone puts you down so you feel that unless you fight you will lose respect or power?

2. How about if someone tries to make you do what you don't want to do? Don't you fight (or argue) to get back your sense of freedom, to do what you want to do, not what someone else wants you to do?

3. Don't you fight because someone rejects you, as when a friend throws you over for someone else? Don't adults fight a lot about love?

4. Don't you hate to hang around people who never laugh or have any fun? Don't you sometimes choose to get nasty and start an argument or a fight just to get away from these dull people?

If, after a short discussion of the above questions, they see your point, ask, "How would you avoid a fight?" For example, "How would you avoid a fight with someone who calls you a bad name?" After a discussion, you might suggest, "If you believe that you are an important person, is it possible to choose to say to the person who called you a bad name that you don't need him, that what he says means nothing to you? Could you say that you think he has a problem, not you, you are doing fine, you have plenty of friends and respect? Why should I waste my time worrying about what you call me, who cares, who are you to me? Nobody."

What you are trying to teach here is that, if we are satisfied with our lives, if we have power, friends, and enough freedom, what does being called a bad name matter? Isn't fighting what you do when you are not sure of yourself? Try to teach that the best way to get along and to avoid fighting, which could get you into serious trouble, is to do all you can to satisfy your needs.

Also, isn't your choice to fight or not to fight the same as choosing not to let someone provoke you? If you let someone provoke you, he, not you, is in control of your life. Ask, "Is it smart to let another person control you by letting him provoke you?" Try to teach them that no one can take away from you what you have unless you let them. You have the power to choose not to fight and not to get into trouble. If someone puts you down, can't you say, "That's your opinion, not mine, and mine is better than yours." Review the process and tell the students that they can put what they have learned into practice. It is new, it takes time, and you will help them, by using these needs and the choices they make when they are frustrated to teach them how not to fight and argue when they are frustrated.

Tell them that what you have begun to teach them is control theory, which is a theory of how they always try to control their lives to best satisfy the five needs that you have been trying to teach them. Tell them that they can put what they have learned into practice in their lives. Ask them if they want to talk further about this theory, and tell them that the more they learn, the better they will be able to control their lives, and the happier they will be.

This is just a small sample of what you can do, as you teach, to introduce control theory into your students' lives. You will find it interesting and worthwhile, and you will get better at it as you do it over and over for a few years. I realize that this hypothetical discussion is just another one of the many suggestions that I have made in this book to try to help you to become a Quality School teacher. What you choose to do may vary somewhat from what I have written here. If you have difficulty teaching control theory to your students, write to me. I will be happy to give you advice on this and on any other suggestion in this book.

CHAPTER TWELVE

Ungraded Quality Assignments

A school is not a Quality School until all the students are doing some quality work. It does not have to be much in the beginning, but it has to be a minimum of one major educational project spread over the school year that both the students and their teachers, in consultation, believe is quality schoolwork. When this should begin in a school committed to becoming a Quality School would be up to individual teachers, but I suggest that a teacher is ready to assign the first quality project as soon as he or she believes that he or she has (1) significantly reduced coercion and is on warm and friendly terms with all students; (2) made a definite start toward teaching only useful work and eliminated rote memory from any evaluations of that work; and (3) begun to teach students to evaluate their own work.

If you are a secondary school teacher, the project would be assigned in only one class, usually an academic class. You would have to get together with the other teachers to make sure that in the beginning only one quality project was assigned. This is important because, for most students, this will be the first time they have attempted such a project. If too much is assigned, they may grow discouraged. The attempt is for the students to see the first project as an opportunity to enjoy doing something they believe is worthwhile that they have never done before in school.

I have talked extensively to elementary and secondary school students about doing such a project. Though it is hard for them to conceptualize something they have never done, almost all have agreed that it seems to be something they would want to try. I begin my discussion by asking if there is any school project or lesson they have done in the past that, when they think about it now, it seems to them to have been a quality project. In most cases they easily remember what they did, are very proud of it, and want to talk about it. When they describe it, which they are very capable of doing even if it took place many years ago, their faces light up, and it is easy to see that it was a highlight of their academic school career. Even though it was not assigned as a quality project, as they recall it in our discussion, it turned out that way.

When I then ask if they would be willing to do something like this again, they are interested. What I have done is make some specific suggestions, and they have agreed that what I suggest is well worth trying. I will describe what I have suggested, and you can try it as described or try to do it your way. Please modify my suggestions as you see fit. Keep in mind that what is needed is for your students to experience doing quality schoolwork. Without tangible evidence of work of this caliber, it is meaningless to talk about a Quality School.

In both elementary and secondary school, I suggested to the students that they select something they wanted to learn and then, proceeding mostly on their own but using the teacher or parent or tutor as a consultant, work on it. They should continue working until, after many self-evaluations (**SESIR**; see chapter nine), they believe that what they have done is quality work. The subject area should be open. I tell them that they can choose anything at all, as long as they are capable of learning about it and showing in some way that they have learned enough so that what they have done has, in their opinion, been a high-quality, enjoyable experience.

In high school the project could cross over subject lines, and the students could ask several teachers to act as consultants. In elementary school, their own teacher would be the major consultant. In both instances, they should be encouraged to choose anyone who was interested in the project and who wanted to help. The more people they involve, the more they will learn; talking to an interested person about what you are doing is one of the best ways to learn a lot about anything. The assignment would be to work on the project until they believe that what they have done is quality. Determining how to show it was quality would be up to them, and deciding it was finished would also be up to them. The teacher would help but not provide too much direction.

Where this project would differ markedly from the usual schoolwork would be that it would not be graded. As long as they could show that a lot of thought and work had gone into it, and provide some evidence that they had done quite a few evaluations as they went along, the project would be acceptable. The idea is to try to teach them that there is usefulness and joy in learning something they are interested in, and that a grade is not needed. I recognize that both students and teachers are leery of ungraded schoolwork, but students have told me they would be willing to try. After we talk, they seem to be able to see the rationale of no grade and of learning for the sake of learning.

I also suggest that this can also be done as a cooperative assignment. If it is cooperative, I think that for the first project, no more than two students should work together. Later, if this becomes a regular procedure, three or four students could be encouraged to work together, but no more than two the first time. Each student would keep a record of what he or she contributed so that there was no doubt that it was cooperative, not one doing most of the work and the other copying.

There should be no strict time limit on the project. It might not even be finished in one school year. What would be necessary is that there be meetings with the project teacher, or consultant if it were someone else, to check on the progress of the project. Finishing it would not be as important as getting into it and having the experience of doing quality work. As Deming would say, constant improvement is the key to quality, and what we would be trying to teach is that quality is really never finished.

What we are trying to get students in a Quality School to understand is that intellectual growth is achieved not so much by finishing something and then going on to something else but by continuing to think about it and work on it. What students need to learn is the process of quality; once they learn that, the products will follow. If they do not learn the process, which is what I am trying to describe here, they will never achieve the products. This is what is so wrong with our schools now: The students do the work and get it done, but the way they do it, the process, rarely involves quality.

Eventually, projects like these will become a major part of the curriculum of a Quality School, but this first project should not be made a requirement. If it is properly presented, most students will accept it. If it works and many students who volunteered begin to enjoy doing it and start to talk about how much fun it is, the nonvolunteers would become interested and would be encouraged to get started. There should be no penalty for not starting, and no one should say "I told you so" when they get going. Only after it proved to be successful should these quality nongraded projects be presented to the students for them to agree that they be made a requirement of the Quality School. Before we worry about this step, we need a lot more data about how this will work out in practice. Generally, students should not have to be required to work in a Quality School; they should want to work. A project like this is a good test of whether a Quality School has been able to accomplish this.

PILOT PROJECTS

Many students will have difficulty figuring out a project, and they will need help. If they select something that is too hard to research or turns out to be less interesting than they think, they should be encouraged to reevaluate and select another project. No student should be locked into something that he or she is not interested in pursuing. Part of learning is to find this out. It may take several starts until a student finally finds something worth working on. Again, the process or system is more important than the product.

Let's say that a high school student picks a project like keeping weapons off school campuses. He could research how it is done in many schools now; he could learn how to make out a questionnaire for students, teachers, and parents at his school and then learn to make sense of the results. He could interview police and politicians about their views on the subject and also find out about the technology of gun detection. He could talk to his consultant to figure out how best to publicize what he has learned and might even lead a discussion in a school assembly about this sensitive topic. He might

146

go to another school or schools to try to get an action program going in a group of schools based on what he found out.

A project like this could easily take a school year, maybe more. He would have to learn about packaging his findings and publicizing them, which would give him a chance to develop his writing skills and use what artistic aptitude he may have. The social studies and history aspects would be obvious. Science could come into play as he investigated how metal detectors and other apparatus worked, and what it would all cost would involve economics. All teachers would be potential consultants, and he would see that what he has learned and is still learning is very useful.

A fourth grader could decide to study dental health and would have to research a variety of things, from diet to toothpaste to fluoride. The cost and availability of dentists would also be studied, and how other countries deal with this problem would be an important part of the research. She could finally come up with some recommendations as to how we need to change so that our system is more responsive to our needs.

I offer these samples only to show that what I am talking about could become a major part of their schooling. It is not so much that the first projects would be this big; the progression would be from small to very large, even multiyear, undertakings. The effort would be not only to understand the process of quality but to get them involved in something that might change the course of their lives. The whole point of a Quality School is to persuade them to see that school is a place where, if they are willing to learn what they are asked to learn, the quality of their lives will improve. Very few students see this now. The need for almost all of them to see this is desperate. If you agree, I'll help you all I can.

Summary

You are engaged in a new process. It will not be easy, but it can be done. The reward for doing it is that you and your students will find that you enjoy what you do together, and the quality of your life and theirs will substantially increase.

A Final Note

Recently, a teacher in Michigan handed me a letter after I finished making a presentation on the Quality School. He said he was part of a faculty almost all of whom would never be interested in implementing the Quality School ideas but that he very much was. He went on to say he believed he was already doing enough in his class of what I recommend in this book and *The Quality School* so that he should be officially designated as leading a Quality Class. He then went on to describe much of what he is doing and there was no doubt that he was very close to, if not already, running such a class.

As I thought about his request, it seemed reasonable. There are probably hundreds of teachers like him who have no chance of ever teaching in a Quality School but who are believers and users of the ideas and want some recognition for what they are doing. Although this book is aimed at teachers who teach in schools that have made the commitment to try to become Quality Schools,

I am sure it will be read by many more than these teachers. What I would like to offer teachers like him is what he requests: If, from your self-evaluation of what is going on in your class or classes, you believe you are leading a Quality Classroom, I would like to hear from you. If I agree with you, I am willing to award some kind of a certificate that you can post on your wall stating that fact.

To support your contention that you are leading a Quality Classroom, I would like you to send me at least the following:

1. Since the Quality School concepts are based on control theory, please send a summary of how you learned control theory and how you are using it in both your life and your work. This is important because knowing and using control theory is what sets a Quality School or Classroom apart from all other school programs.

2. A description of how you handle all classroom problems and situations noncoercively by talking to your students with emphasis on warm support from you and from each other. Tell me a little about how you reveal yourself to your students.

3. Examples of how you explain the usefulness of what you teach and how you know that your students accept what you ask them to do as useful. I am especially interested in how you have eliminated the usual required memorization.

4. How you are putting concurrent evaluation, with student teaching assistants helping, into your class, as well as any other example of how your students have been evaluating their own work.

5. A statement from each student supportive of what you are doing.

6. A sample of one piece of quality work from each student if you teach in a self-contained class. Use your judgment regarding how many samples of quality work to send if you are a secondary school teacher with many students.

7. Supportive parent evaluations of what you are doing.

8. Anything else that you believe documents what you are doing that has made your classroom a Quality Classroom.

If you are able to do this and you have worked at least two and a half years in reaching this point, I am willing to designate you as a Quality Classroom Teacher. What form this will take has yet to be worked out but I am excited by the prospect of many teachers working for this designation. You could be the catalyst that persuades other teachers in your school to turn in this direction. Also, this designation could be shown to the hiring person of a contract school if the time comes when you want to move to a place where there is real support for what you are trying to do.

Please note that this offer is not open to teachers in schools that have signed the contract and are working as a whole school to become a Quality School. When that occurs, every teacher in the school will be designated as a Quality Teacher in the now Quality School. It would be divisive and unproductive to award separate certificates of classroom quality to the teachers in a contract school ahead of the school itself being designated a Quality School. This is a way to augment the use of the ideas, not to change the basic idea, which is to get whole schools involved. If you have any questions please get in touch with the institute.

Notes

1. Lloyd Dobyns and Clare Crawford-Mason, *Quality or Else,* Houghton Mifflin, Boston, MA, 1991.

2. A brief but adequate explanation of control theory is in my 1990 book, *The Quality School.* More detailed information is in my 1984 book, *Control Theory.* All my books are published by HarperCollins, New York, NY.

3. For information on how your school can become a member of the Quality School Consortium and about the contract that the staff principal and staff members need to sign to join, see the Author's Note at the beginning of this book.

4. See William Glasser, *The Control Theory Manager,* HarperCollins, New York, NY, 1993.

5. "A Day with Dr. Deming," sponsored by the Chief of Naval Operations, December 20, 1991, and published by the Office of the Chief of Naval Operations, The Pentagon, Room 4E522, Washington, D.C. 20350-2000.

6. Ibid.

7. Ibid.

8. Ibid.

9. In the world of business, management and labor are just now (thirty years too late) beginning to see that quality, not just competence, is what is needed if businesses are to compete successfully.

10. Materials written to assist in teaching control theory to students:

Grade	Program	Publisher
1 & 2	*Teach Them to Be Happy,* Robert Sullo	New View Publications P.O. Box 3021 Chapel Hill, NC 27515
3 & 4	*My Quality World,* Carleen Floyd	New View Publications
5	*Off to Be the Wizard,* Marilyn Crawford	New View Publications
6	"Choice"	Educator Training Center 117 East Eighth St., Suite 810 Long Beach, CA 90813

7 & 8   "In Pursuit of Happiness" New View
        Perry Good   Publications

        Guidebook for   New View
          In Pursuit of Happiness Publications
        Delores Haberman

For parents and staff, the books and materials for discussion and knowledge are:

The Quality School   Institute for Reality Therapy
Dr. William Glasser   7301 Medical Center Dr.
                          Suite 104
                          Canoga Park, CA 91307

In Pursuit of Happiness New View Publications
Perry Good

Helping Kids Help   New View Publications
  Themselves
Perry Good

Restitution   New View Publications
Diane Gossen

My Child Is a Pleasure   New View Publications
  to Live With
Diane Gossen